CREATIVE SILENCE

CREATIVE SILENCE
Through Inner Silence to the Harvest of the Spirit

by

DENIS DUNCAN

An Amulree Paperback

No. 1

published by
ARTHUR JAMES LIMITED
The Drift, Evesham,
Worcs., England

First Edition 1980

© Denis Duncan 1980

Duncan, Denis
Creative Silence.
— (Amulree paperbacks).
1. Devotion
I. Title
II. Series
248'.3 BV4815
ISBN 0-85305-222-0

Printed by **Gibbons Barford** Wolverhampton

PREFACE

This little book consists of two series of articles written for my weekly devotional contributions to *British Weekly*. Permission to use that material in this way has generously been given by David Coomes, the Editor of that journal, and I acknowledge that courtesy with gratitude.

My publisher has asked me to write on the bases of the devotional life in such a way that it will be understood by everybody and especially by those unused to material on spirituality. This is a difficult and a risky task! It is difficult because the very nature of the material is in the area of (to use the Pauline phrase to which I have referred several times in the text) 'the knowledge which is beyond knowledge' (Ephesians 3:19, *New English Bible*). It will therefore always be true that those who have ears to hear will hear, but others will be puzzled and disappointed by what they try to read. To the latter, I apologise in advance. It is also a risky task because it probably puts me on 'a hiding to nothing'! I will not satisfy the academic or the theologian who may find this contribution naive, and yet, because the theme is one of depth, I may well not satisfy the 'ordinary' reader who could find it hard to 'latch on' to what I am trying to convey. I suggest anyone finding themselves in this latter category turn to the theme 'Peace' in The Harvest of the Spirit section and read on from there to the end, then returning to the beginning and trying again! If nobody finds it satisfying then my publisher will not be pleased either!

I trust however that I may say some things that are of help. I have used material of this kind in preaching, lecturing and healing ministry services and there have been indications of blessing received through it. I hope it will stimulate many in their devotional life.

This book is no more than an introduction to the themes it covers. Every chapter could be — and I hope in due time many of them will be — books in themselves. This is especially true of the various 'fruits of the Spirit' — 'Love' for example will be such a book in the not too distant future, so it is no more than mentioned in the pages allocated to it in this one. I have not attempted a systematic or comprehensive survey of the matters raised. I sought simply to do what I try to do in my weekly devotional articles, stimulate the life of the soul and minister to the 'inner being' in an age which needs renewed emphasis on the spiritual and demands that Christians take 'life in the Spirit' seriously. It is my prayer that I have made a tiny contribution to this.

A companion volume of 'Thoughts and Prayers for Each Day of a Year' under the title *A Day at a Time* is being published as near simultaneously as possible. Enquiry about it can be addressed to Arthur James Limited. That is based on the 'Saturday Prayers' used in my weekly diary column in *British Weekly* and on other prayers, plus a thought for each day from my writing in that journal, which is published by Christian Weekly Newspapers from 146 Queen Victoria Street, London E.C. 4.

Quotations from the Bible are from the *Authorised Version* unless specifically noted as NEB, that is the *New English Bible*, or WB, that is *William Barclay's* translation.

I am grateful to my friend, Arthur Ingham, who has designed the cover, and to Jillian Tallon for her devoted help in typing and retyping my material.

DENIS DUNCAN

CONTENTS

Cover designed by Arthur Ingham

CREATIVE SILENCE

Through Inner Silence to the Harvest of the Spirit

PROLOGUE

The bus conductress — 'a character' as so many Glaswegian transport staff are — was very angry. The commuters were trying to get home. The football crowd was on its way to the match. There was much pushing and jostling, and she lost her temper. In stentorian Glasgow tones she screamed: 'For goodness sake, come on, get off!'

Taken literally, the command is an impossible one, but there is paradox as well as contradiction in the words — at least if you apply the statement to the church, for the church is — or ought to be — a body, *coming and going, at the same time.* 'Come unto me.' It is the body which comes together in worship for Christ's sake. 'Go ye into all the world.' It is at the same time the body which is called to go out in His name.

The church is less than Christ's church if it omits either half of the paradox. A church which 'comes' but does not 'go' will end up a pious club. A church which is always on the 'go' may come to be no more than social service, out of touch with the base from which it operates as Christ's church. For that reason, the twin commitments of the church, Christ's people, are to 'retreat' and 'involvement' — together.

INTRODUCTION

'Retreat' and 'involvement' must always be held together in the life of the church and in the lives of Christian disciples. As in so many other areas of Christian living, apparently paradoxical emphases must remain intimately related if true balance is to be attained. Christian thinking has suffered when over-emphasis or, even more, exclusive emphasis has been put on one side of the paradoxes that are our efforts to express the infinite in finite thoughts and words.

There is, for example, always danger when we leave out 'objectivity' in our determination of Christian truth, and rely solely on 'subjectivity'. The truth involves both our experience — the 'subjective' element — and the testing of that experience against some 'objective' standard. That objective standard is, for me, the record of the experience of God's people in history, personal and corporate; in other words, 'the Word of God'.

To take another paradox, Christianity is highly 'individual' and wholly corporate or 'communal' — and both components in that paradox must be emphasised in balance and in proper relationship. The fundamental question of faith is a personal one and it demands an *individual* response. 'Whom say *ye* that I am?' Jesus asked his disciples (Matthew 16:15ff). That personal response made, the decision involves joining oneself to the company of people — the church — who similarly have confessed: 'Thou art the Christ, the Son of the living God', in order to have opportunity to express faith in witness, work and worship and undertake the responsibilities of discipleship — proclamation, fellowship and service.

This is a book which is more about 'retreat' than 'involvement'. 'Involvement' is however implicit in all that I say in trying to describe the implications of partnership with the Spirit. This partnership is developed in the 'inner silence' and expressed beautifully in Paul's phrase, 'the Fruits of the Spirit', or, as the *New English Bible* renders it, 'the Harvest of the Spirit'. For 'involvement' in the life of the world through ministry, witness and service, can only come out of 'retreat'.

I have been greatly concerned with 'involvement' in my ministry. The journal in which the material on which I am basing this book — *British Weekly* — was, as its great founder Sir William Robertson Nicoll intended it to be, a crusading newspaper expounding the Christian Gospel in the life of the world, and in my own period as its Editor, I endeavoured to maintain that 'involvement'. But there has been — for me and I think the church in general — too much 'involvement' and too little 'retreat' in my years in the ministry. As a result the church, genuinely endeavouring to serve a world in need, has not always stayed close enough to the source of its life, namely a full living partnership with the Spirit. Without this its life and work can only be superficial and its message diluted.

There will be much to be said about 'involvement' at some other time. Here I concern myself with the ground of our life and witness, that which I am summing up in the word 'retreat'. But perhaps the word 'retreat' as popularly used, is misleading. It sounds like escaping! It isn't. It is, as the dictionary rightly defines it, a 'period of seclusion'. In other words, we 'retreat' for a purpose. We 'retreat' in order to be more 'involved'.

The Iona Community has demonstrated this admirably over many years. Its members 'retreat' each year to the holy island of Iona, the very fountainhead of Celtic Christianity in Scotland through St. Columba, to be renewed and regenerated through prayer, fellowship and work. Then each would return to his place of ministry. For Iona Community members this was almost universally a hard, tough assignment — in shipyard, new town, down-town slum, etc. 'Retreat' was the launching pad for yet more 'involvement'.

My aim in this devotional study is to deal with the 'deep roots and firm foundations' of the inward life through the theme of creative inner silence, and then to outline the harvest of the Spirit, the produce in the real world of that silence where partnership with the Spirit is discovered and developed to the glory of God and for the good of people.

PART
1

The Christian Map

THE CHRISTIAN takes his stance *within* the faith. He starts from certain fundamental statements that cannot, in the ordinary sense of the words, be proved. In other words he starts from facts he knows only 'by revelation'. St. Paul, in his letter to the Galatians, states this unambiguously. 'The Gospel which I preach is no human affair. I owe my knowledge to no man's instruction and to no man's teaching. No! It came to me by direct revelation from Jesus Christ.' (Galatians 1:11–12, WB). Jesus adds His authority to the reality of this 'knowledge which is beyond knowledge' (Ephesians 3:19, NEB) when, in response to Peter's confession of Him as 'the Son of the living God', He says: 'Flesh and blood hath not revealed it unto thee, but my Father which is in Heaven' (Matthew 16:17).

This does not make for easy discussion in matters of Christian faith, or in the defence of faith. Religious discussion usually follows the pattern of all other human discussion and is expressed in terms of logic, proof, rationality, etc. If faith was a matter of mental or rational understanding only, that method and process would be the natural one to follow. But faith is not limited in this way. Faith deals with the infinite, not the finite, with the divine as well as the human, with the soul and the spirit as well as the mind. To say 'Jesus is Lord' in the sense of the great Christian statements of belief, is to say things about Jesus that can never, at a human level and in a human way, be 'proved'. Belief in the Incarnation of our Lord and the Resurrection and Ascension of our Lord, who is, we say, 'Son of God', lies beyond logic and proof. Belief in the Holy Spirit as a living energy and active force in personal life will seem only to be fantasy to the scientific mind, so statements like 'I believe in the Holy Spirit' must appear 'irrational' to those outside Christian faith. They are statements of faith about facts which no finite, human system of words and concepts can confirm or deny. Yet they are 'facts' so far as the Christian is concerned.

We find ourselves, therefore, taking up a stance that is based on reality for us but may well be fantasy, imagination or autosuggestion, for those who cannot accept the concept of the 'knowledge which is beyond knowledge'. But we can 'do no other'. It is from this stance that we construct our 'map', the map on which we base all that we do, say and are in Christian terms.

I use the word 'map' in this context to describe the product of that body of knowledge (both rational and intuitional) *and* experience in relation to which we decide our direction in life and run our course. It is not something immutably fixed (maps do change over the years), but it is the stable structure, built on faith and revealed knowledge, in which change is more likely to be in detail rather than in essence. The 'map' is our philosophy of life. It includes the fundamental presuppositions without which we cannot find meaning in life. And, because the stance we take is one in which we feel bound to 'look unto Jesus' as 'the author and finisher of our faith', the map that we evolve is one that is properly called 'Christian'.

Is there, however, such a thing as '*the* Christian map'? Or can we only talk of '*a* Christian map', i.e. one among several possible maps? At one time people would have felt quite at ease in talking of 'the' Christian map, and would have simply quoted a credal statement as that map or offered the 'authorised' faith of the Church. But at a time when the demand is that we be 'honest to God' and make up our own minds; when every possible component of the Christian's faith has been brought into question — and not by hostile critics only, but from within the churches themselves (as in the 'death of God' phase), it is less easy to be dogmatic about any Christian map offered. I can only state then the elements *I* feel crucial to *my* Christian map and hope that 'deep speaks to deep'. I therefore make this personal statement of the basis on which I approach the theme of this book. I hope this (as I believe it to be) 'essential Christianity' strikes a chord with those who read this volume for it is the ground on which I found the development of 'the life of the Spirit' through the 'inner silence' (which is a 'creative silence') and show its product — or produce — to be the 'fruit of the Spirit', 'the harvest of the Spirit'.

I believe in God the Father, in Jesus Christ — incarnate, crucified, risen and 'alive', and in the gift of the Holy Spirit, 'abiding with us for ever'. I believe that that which is summed up, formally, as 'the doctrine of the Trinity' is a majestic human effort to express, in rounded statement, the experience of the church and of each individual of the loving God who has made Himself known in Christ, through the Spirit.

There are other tenets of belief and conviction I should add if I were formulating a full 'credo', but all that I am concerned to state here is that 'the Christian map' by which I set our course is also one that involves — and indeed cannot do without — the dimension which is summed up in the word 'Spirit' with a capital 'S'.

That capital 'S' is crucial. There is so much contemporary confusion in the words 'spirit' and 'spiritual' that I quote, with great appreciation, the point made by Paul Tillich in his *Systematic Theology*, volume I: 'The term 'spiritual' (with a lower-case 's') must be sharply distinguished from 'Spiritual' (with a capital 'S'). The latter refers to activities of the Divine Spirit in man; the former to the dynamic-creative nature of man's personal and collective life'.

It is 'Spirit' with a capital 'S' that is definitive for all I have to say. It is the fundamental feature for me on the Christian's map and it is to be in touch with that Spirit that we go into the inner silence. It is as a result of contact with that Spirit that the harvest of the Spirit comes.

We are partners with the Spirit, and it is in 'creative' silence that that partnership is sealed.

*   *   *

From this specific stance it follows that there are quite fundamental ways in which we shall look at both personality and reality so it is important that I state these now.

First, *personality*. It is integral to the argument of this book that man (and to save unnecessary repetition, I shall use 'man', 'his', etc., throughout as generic terms to describe all humanity) is a being who has physical, emotional, mental and spiritual aspects in his life and that his wholeness involves all these parts. They are inter-related and inter-dependent so that health or its opposite 'dis-ease' in any one 'area' may affect the health of the whole or any other part, for good or ill-ness. Man is therefore body, mind, heart (using that word to indicate the seat of the emotions) and soul or spirit, and his life, in satisfaction and fulfilment terms, depends on the growth and development of all these parts together and in balance with each other. The 'spirit' or 'soul' part dare not be neglected. It is therefore at this point we take our departure from those theoretical systems or models which recognise only body, mind and heart, but not 'soul'.

There is, however, a further important matter of stance to be established firmly and here I return to the point made by Paul Tillich which I quoted earlier. There are many approaches to wholeness that make 'spirit' with a lower-case 's' very important but do not recognise or give validity to 'Spirit' with a capital 'S'. They therefore recognise (to quote Tillich) 'the dynamic-creative nature of man's personal and collective life' but do not go on to recognise also the essential factor on which the thesis of this book depends, namely the crucial component of the 'activities of the Divine Spirit in man'. This leads such people to make statements that are true in themselves, statements to which one can give complete agreement — for example that to be in a loving or caring relationship is to be involved in a 'spiritual' undertaking. That is true, but the Christian stance I am taking makes it all-important to go further than this. The integration of the human personality is, in my view, impossible without the 'activity of the Holy Spirit'. This is fundamental to our view of the aims of life and their fulfilment through personality.

The second point relates to our view of *reality*. It is the popular attitude of 'the world' to see 'reality' as the things that can be seen, touched, handled, etc. Brought up in and conditioned by scientific and technological attitudes, it has been normal, for many generations, to see reality as the 'material'. It may well be that that statement applies less to present and immediately future generations for there are many signs — from physics as well as from faith — that a 'new age of the spiritual' is coming to pass. I do not define this in over-optimistic terms but there are so many 'straws in the wind' (and 'wind' and 'Spirit' are the same words in Hebrew and Greek) that such a statement is possible. That said, the 'conditioning' of us all has been of that 'materialistic' kind and 'reality' is therefore for most of us, that of which the senses are aware.

The *Christian* map is however, based on that important statement of Paul's in his second letter to the Corinthians, chapter 4. He writes: 'While we look not at the things which are seen, but at the things which are not seen: for the things which are seen are temporal, but the things which are not seen are eternal' (verse 18). 'Reality' from the Christian perspective is the opposite of the 'worldly' perspective, and this is fundamental to the Christian view of life. Life in the world must be seen *sub specie aeternitatis* — that is in the context of a life that reaches beyond this world. To attach 'reality' only to the physical part of the body and the material world is to set limits that are wholly 'unreal'! The growth and development of the Christian must therefore be based, not on the limited view of human personality offered by science or psychology, but on the view evident in the very nature of Christ Himself as well as in His words — that He came from the spiritual sphere to be incarnate for a time in this physical, material world of flesh and body in order to fulfil a mission; that He returned to that greater sphere (the doctrines of resurrection and ascension) where the 'corruptible must put on incorruption and this mortal must put on immortality' for 'flesh and blood cannot inherit the Kingdom of God' (I Corinthians 15:50, 53).

Jesus, when He prayed for His disciples (John 17), prayed that they should be 'in' the world but not 'of' it. How to live 'in' the world and within it, produce 'the harvest of the Spirit' is the theme of this book. The way to that harvest is through inner silence, the silence that is 'Creative Silence', the silence in which we come to know 'the activity of the Spirit'.

2
The Need for Silence

TO BE TRULY silent is one of the hardest things in *our* world! It is a world so conditioned to noise, words and activity that silence tends to be dismissed as an irrelevance or classified as inertia. It has little place in the accepted 'busy-ness' of life. It is not valued by those who make an idol of 'involvement'. It is therefore usually consigned to the area of 'retreat'.

The dismissal of silence so summarily to the traditional place of retreat, the desert is, in a sense, to make a public assessment of its unimportance. To confine it to the desert suggests that it is not for the ordinary but only for the extra-ordinary, not for the man-in-the-street but for the monk-in-the-cell, not for the pragmatist but for the mystic, not for the activist but for the dreamer. The present popularity of retreat, personal and corporate, suggests that a lesson is being learned, however. It is that the need to minister to the inner life is a general and not a specialist need. It is moreover the fundamental need in humanity seen in terms of our Christian map. Ministry to the soul, the development of the spiritual and therefore contact with the Spirit provides the breath the Christian needs to live as a child of God. Silence, the capacity to be still and listen, is a 'categorical imperative' of the Christian life. Without the development of the life of the soul through the silence, we cannot attain to 'fullness of being, the fullness of God Himself' (Ephesians 3:19, NEB). Silence is, for the soul, wholly creative and it is through creative, inner silence that we are enabled to begin to produce the harvest of the Spirit.

One of the problems of commitment to silence is the demand it makes in this noise-dominated world. It is not easy to live with silence if you are most at home with noise. So silence is little recognised, for deliberately living with noise, is a characteristic of our time. Students work with radios on. 'Transistors' are carried on walks, taken on journeys and generally treated as part of the paraphernalia without which life is impossible. Leisure is often time spent listening to noisy programmes in discos, on records and tapes or in clubs. Television mutters on as a background to conversation come what — or who — may. (Pastoral visitation has found this a real problem of life today!)

Even in churches, the normal is to concentrate on words. There are (rightly) always sermons in services, but rarely silence; always words, rarely meditative listening; often discussion groups, rarely groups for silent contemplation. Having expressed the value and need for silence in worship, the leader of the service in one church intimated that there would now be ten seconds' silence. Ten seconds! That is not silence: it is a catch in the breath! Creative silence is real silence, real attention, real listening, real adoration.

'Be still and know that I am God' (Psalm 46:10). There is the call to the desert here.

*　　　*　　　*

'To go to the desert is to return to the source.' So wrote a modern saint to remind us that the creation of the opportunity for silence, in order that it may be creative silence, involves a journey. The journey is one of exploration, of adventure and of risk. It is a seeking, searching, yearning undertaking in which the longing of the soul for true stillness is paramount.

The desert, using that word literally, has been the kind of place where men sought and found God. It has been the sanctuary of the saints and the true home of holy men. It was the place to which our Lord went. *Driven by the Spirit*, He remained there forty days and forty nights, fasting. There, in the silence of the desert, He met the Tempter, head-on. There in the solitude of the desert, He 'heard' the subtle suggestions that struggled within Him, persuading Him to use His divine gifts for personal or national glory. Material gain (stones could be made bread), divine magic (angelic protection in physical danger), glory and power (to the extent of universal dominion) were all possible, if only He would surrender to the subtle, sinister seduction of such promptings. It was in the silence of the desert that contributed to His own inner silence, that He could summon up the strength of spirit (ministered to by the Spirit Himself), to reject, for ever, the prostitution of the divinity He felt within Him.

There was St. Paul. He went to Arabia to consider profound questions that he had to face (Galatians 1:17). He felt the need for the kind of silence only the desert can provide. There he could find his own creative, inner silence, and work out his mission in Christ's name.

What is it about the desert that brings such nurture to the soul? It is the opportunity for silence, without *and* within. The noise of the world will disappear there. Silence appreciated creates silence within. The opportunity to listen and 'hear' the voice of the Lord comes in the desert. In other words, the desert brings communication in relationship — our relationship to God — to a deeper level. The capacity for awareness is heightened. It is not that we cannot hear the word of the Lord in the market-place or the city. There is just too much distraction there to draw the mind to the things of the soul. If the soul is to be truly fed, the opportunity to 'look unto Jesus' single-mindedly is essential. We must 'be still' to know. . . .

There is a paradox here, as there is so often in the things of the faith — as we have already seen. Christianity is focussed on community. The Church is made up of people. Our need however is to get away from people, *for a time*, in order to serve and love them more. 'Retreat' (as

I said in the introduction) is essential to 'involvement'. Soul-searching precedes soul-serving. The call of the desert is a primal call in 'the life of the Spirit'.

But there is more to be said about the desert. It is, in some way, *the place of abandonment*. It is concerned with life, but life without so much 'the world' regards as essential. The desert is the place of greater self-understanding, of deepening self-awareness, and so of sensitivity to the relationship between our crying needs and the 'smiling Providence' ready to offer response in grace. In the desert we draw nearer that part of us that is swamped by duties and work, social intercourse, superficial undertaking, sophistication and 'civilisation', hurry and haste, speed and stress. Sadly all that we have to do, including the many good things we undertake, can stifle the soul, its needs and its potential.

Affluence breeds spiritual danger. It is hard for a rich man to enter the Kingdom of God (cf. Luke 18:24). Sophistication snuffs out the essential simplicity required by the student member of God's Realm. 'Except ye ... become as little children, ye shall not enter the Kingdom of Heaven' (Matthew 18:3). The needs of the soul demand the abandonment of most of what is normal to 'the world' and command a stripping down of us all to the true realities of life, defined in terms of the Christian map and recognised in the life of the Spirit.

This cannot happen without silence. The desert is the place where, distractions destroyed and self laid bare, it is possible to begin to 'press toward the mark for the prize of the high calling of God in Christ Jesus' (Philippians 3:14). To find this creative opportunity, explorers of the silence down the ages have taken the road to the desert.

The desert need not be the sandy wastes or mountain bleakness of the locations in which our Lord and St. Paul found the solitude, simplicity and silence that they needed to determine their spiritual courses, the place of abandonment that was essential to their inward being.

There must, however, be, in the life of the pilgrim who is eager to know and 'practise the Presence of God', some symbolic 'desert place' to which to go. It may be some sanctuary hallowed by the ages. It may be some natural place of beauty that speaks of the things of the Spirit. It may be a home-made sanctuary in some upper or back room in the place where you live. It matters not, so long as it is the kind of place in which silence is possible, the 'still, small voice' can be heard, the inner self may be known, and the presence of God be felt real and active. That place can be the most important place in life for it is there, in the silence of one's own chosen 'desert place' that the struggle for the life of the soul will be fought, and the battle for the salvation of that soul can be won. What happens when 'deep speaks to deep' in the inner silence, when soul is touched by Spirit, will 'save' the whole person, me, us, all. For it is as whole persons, unified beings, God deals with us, and it is by grace, we unified, whole beings 'are saved through faith'.

Let the Spirit then speak to that part of us which reaches out for the divine, our souls. Let silence reign, so that the Spirit can come when we are silent within. In that creative, inner silence, the miracle of grace is wrought.

But before we go on to the struggle of the silence there are some things that must be said about the search for inner silence.

*   *   *

Learning *how* to be silent is crucial to the growth and development of the inner life. If the process of 'sanctification', or growth in Christian character, is to take place; if the balance between spirit and flesh is to be found; if serenity, tranquillity and calmness of mind are to be nurtured; if the harvest of the Spirit is to evolve, contact with the Holy Spirit is essential. That Divine Spirit is not limited. It 'bloweth where it listeth' and is not confined to one method of contact. Indeed one can be very conscious of the presence of the Spirit in the commuter train, in the kitchen, on the battlefield (as many have testified), in the laboratory, in the operating theatre. It is nevertheless true that, to create a life in the Spirit and to develop that life in depth, discipline and commitment are needed. One place of contact with the Spirit is in the silence. So commitment and discipline are essential if we are to receive the blessings of the silence.

If we are going to draw on this divine energy available to us, we have to (as it were) 'stop the world' and 'get off' for a period of time. This (and I repeat what I said about 'retreat') is not escapism of any kind. To 'switch off' from the temporal, visible world is not an 'un-real' process. It is to put oneself in a position where there is contact at a deep level with the 'divine dimension'. That is not to forsake reality but to aim to find it. Reality lies, in terms of our stance and map, in the spiritual, not the temporal, and it is that reality we want to find. Our minds have then a key role to play in the temporary re-alignment of our attentive processes.

All through each day it is the function of our minds to control our thoughts, attention and activities in a way that enables us to survive, to make decisions, to deal with life at levels trivial, less trivial and not trivial; to 'computerise' the information that enables us to function in the world and get us safely through it. The brain is the physical mechanism through which this process is worked out. The mind is the controlling capacity. So we must keep our minds on things if we are to cope with the daily facts and factors of life.

It is not my purpose here to go into the complex relationships and theories that enter into exact definition of these terms. I am only concerned to make one crucial point about the process essential to getting in touch with the inner being, and that is the need to 'still the mind' in order to allow contact with the things of the Spirit. So our minds which, day by day, cope with the thousands of decisions of a practical nature that have to be made, have for a period to lay aside that important, necessary function in order to take up that which is their priority function — to cease concern with the messages of ordinary living in order to be available to messages from the soul.

It is not possible in life to divide our concentration. Of course we can do two things at once, in a superficial sense, but when we really mean 'concentration', we cannot perform two tasks simultaneously. The surgeon carrying out a delicate operation can not, at the same time, be deeply concerned with the problems of his marriage. The pilot, on take-off or landing, dare not, at that time, be concerned with planning a new house. We are either mentally involved to the full in what we are doing or we switch off in order to do something else. So it is with the mind. It must let go of 'worldly' things in order to be open to eternal things.

In terms of stilling the mind and ceasing to concentrate for a period on every day responsibilities, in order to dwell on the things of the soul, it is essential to ensure that we are in the right place and circumstances to do this (which points to the need for 'going into the closet and closing the door' as Jesus advised). The process is a deliberate one and a conscious one. The mind must be stilled to allow it to become the medium of access to the soul and the Spirit, and the conditions must be provided in which this can be done.

The need to be absolutely 'concentrated' in this spiritual exercise was made very real to me early in my ministry when I decided to introduce background organ music into the Communion Service when the elements were (as was the usual practice then in my church) being distributed round the congregation by the elders. The idea seemed helpful and it is indeed common practice, in my experience, in English Nonconformist churches. I abandoned the practice when it was put to me — and I realised it too — that the music was distracting people from the silence; that one could listen to — and be inspired by — *either* the silence *or* the music but it was not possible, in any real way, to do both. You could not 'hear' the silence for the music. This may be personal to me, but enquiry suggests it is not. The mind seriously undertakes one process at a time if concentration is really demanded. When we reach the most profound area of life — the life of the soul — the mind insists on putting away the practicalities of the world before engaging deeply with the profundities of the soul.

'Meditation', as that word is being used today, is a description of that process of 'mind-stilling' with a view to engagement with the Spirit. I say 'as that word is used today' because it is a change of use from popular ideas of 'Meditation'. In church circles it has been used generally of a thinking process — meditation on a theme. What I have been describing is meditation as a *non-thinking* process which is the opposite of the 'normal' use of the word. For it is the need to stop thought and thinking which is of the essence of the search for inner silence.

That does not mean there is no place for thinking and the intellectual in the up-building of the life of the Spirit, but the 'reflection' follows the experience instead of being a substitute for it. In other words we stop thinking so that we may be receptive and open to that which will come to us 'from the other direction', not from 'the world', but from within. Meditation is then an attentive, expectant waiting on the Spirit, who speaks in the soul. It is 'towards' the soul the mind is now concentrated and not the physical or the mental, and it is on that alone that it must be wholly free to concentrate.

I shall return later to some further comments on meditation understood as the way in which, through waiting on God in the silence, we come into touch with the energies of the Spirit, the energies that create the fruit, the harvest of the Spirit. Here I note my reason for describing the inner silence as the 'Creative Silence'. For growth in grace and 'in the likeness of Jesus Christ' can only take place through contact with the energies and influence of the Spirit.

I see this need to be still, to focus the mind in this other direction, to wrestle with the things of the Spirit as a necessary part of every Christian life. Protest will arise on the ground that there is no time in busy households for long periods of meditation and no opportunity for silence — and that is a relevant protest. Meditation does not however have to be seen only in this context. When the ability to still the mind and (as it were) to turn its attention in this other direction has been achieved, it can be done in any situation — in an underground train, on a plane, anywhere. What it is necessary to realise is that the ability to do that arises out of developing the capacity to still the mind, over a period. To do it at will is the result of self-discipline, not a substitute for it.

Before we look at 'the struggle within', may I enter an important caveat in this field.

The practice of inner silence — the form of meditation which I am describing — may not necessarily be the right way for everyone. Indeed for some it may be unhelpful and even dangerous — for this reason. When we stop all our restless 'busy-ness' and feverish mental activity and try to look 'within', we do also open the door to 'material from the unconscious' welling up and making its presence felt. That material may be disturbing, frightening, worrying. If we have the inner strength and security to cope with this, the experience can be a creative one. But if our 'defences' are down, we may simply be overwhelmed by the kind of thoughts we are getting and consequently 'break down'.

That statement draws on understandings we have gained from the work of the great pioneers of psychological understanding — in particular Sigmund

Freud and Carl Jung. It is not our purpose here to go into 'depth psychology' and the analytical approaches that these theories represent. What we can do is acknowledge our debt to these great names in psychology and draw on their discoveries.

As well as the conscious knowledge we have of ourselves and the knowledge others have of us and which can be made available to us, the greatest practical influence on our lives is the knowledge we do not have of ourselves and which others do not have of us either. What others do not know of us and we ourselves do not know is the content of our 'unconscious', that is the great repository of experience within us that affects us in so many ways. This knowledge and experience is, as it is popularly put, 'sub-conscious'. In other words we are not normally aware of it, though in dreams, in analysis, in deep personal sharing in a psychotherapeutic relationship, we can be 'in touch' with some of it.

To be self-aware in this way can be very helpful to us. To come to see why and how we cause irritation, upset, anger in others when we do not know why this happens, is useful. And this is still true when we come to the 'shadow' or negative side of the unconscious. To be aware of our 'bad' parts, the unacceptable parts of ourselves, helps us to face and accept them, to our benefit and gain.

This kind of process of self-awareness is all right when it happens in a specific and defined situation — for example, within a relationship of a professional therapeutic kind, or within a group where 'sharing' leads to 'caring' and support. But if we are alone in our closed closet and this kind of process takes place, we may simply find that, in the silence, and being in touch with our inner selves, things are coming into consciousness — guilt from the past, frustration in the present, depression about the future — which are just too much for us. For that reason it is wise, in early days of meditation of this kind, to meditate in a group, a group in which there is sensitivity, empathy and acceptance.

There is a particular danger in this area for people who are 'off-balance' (and I shall say more on the concept of balance later) psychologically in that, already beset by matter which they cannot handle, the practice of silence can open the floodgates and they are overwhelmed by unacceptable material 'from the unconscious'. A meditation group should be aware of this kind of danger and be able to cope with the effects of it should this sort of upset arise.

Inevitably the stilling of the mind and the closing down of the 'defences' which activity and conscious effort represent can be a time of risk and strain. In psychological work it often is. But I am writing here in the context of the spiritual where there is divine support and protection against negative spiritual attack or pressure. The receptiveness we offer is focussed on positive and creative influence, centred in the presence and power of the Spirit. That attitude of expectation, within a community of grace, will lead, we hope, to inflow of an inspiring and uplifting kind.

That just that happens is the testimony of so many who have explored the inner silence. But I refer deliberately to this possible negative reaction, the result of our humanity, the product of the shadow side of the unconscious and the 'collective unconscious', in order to warn in advance of the risks of isolated soul-searching in the silence without support.

Risk? Yes, indeed. But the risk is the creative risk of freedom. We are, as children of God, free to tamper with the occult or temper life through the Spirit: we can choose black magic or we can seek first the Kingdom of God; we can abuse spiritual awareness or we can gain immeasurably from it. The choice is ours. The choice of creative silence opens the door to so much that can minister to the spiritual life. The question is our readiness to risk new levels of awareness.

Perhaps the great blessings of heightened (or deepened) awareness are illustrated in the story of the walk to Emmaus when two disciples talked theology but failed to realise the presence of the subject of their theological discussion. The Jesus of whom they were speaking was there, but their level of spiritual awareness was low. (There is a point here about the possibility of academic theological discussion preventing the spiritual sense working!) When evening came, something happened that changed that level of awareness totally. 'He was made known to them in the breaking of the bread' (Luke 24:35). That did it! They touched a new level of spiritual sensitivity and they saw the Lord.

Creative silence has to do with the changing of levels of awareness for the inspiration of the soul and, through it, the whole being. It is a glorious world to enter and it is the purpose of this book to encourage you to 'enter here'. I did however want to place the risks on record, for in the realm of the Spirit, we are in touch with cosmic forces that are never neutral. Even in our stillness, even through our silence, the battle waged by the enemy goes on. Before we now discuss that struggle in greater depth, that word of warning was necessary.

3

The Salvation of the Silence

IT IS IN the silence of the desert that the battle for the life or death of the soul will be decided, for there the trivial, the false, the decorative is stripped away and human beings come face to face with themselves and with God. Here the awareness of the great cosmic battle between good and evil is seen as a battle within ourselves too. Here the forces of the Spirit encounter the powers of darkness in our own soul. It is here the conflict rages. It is here the victory will be won. We must therefore seek to be 'in Christ' and have 'Christ in us' in order to exclude the presence of the evil forces that strive to enlist us on the side of anti-Christ.

That is why we must learn of the methods and tactics of the 'evil one', whether we see that agency as 'personal devil' or 'evil force'. For lack of knowledge of the nature, scope and persistence of temptation will lead us to depression over our inner state when no such despair is appropriate.

The place to which we can go in order to see this point clearly is the arena of temptation in which our Lord found Himself at the outset of His ministry. Here the nature of the struggle between good and evil even in the Son of God (and nothing so emphasises that He was truly human than the fact that He endured this same conflict in the most extreme form) is vividly illustrated.

We often despair because temptation can *follow* profound religious experience so closely. We question our sincerity, bemoan our lack of grace and strength. We despair as people without hope because, though we have, for whatever reason, touched a rich vein of spiritual experience, we 'fall' again and again and again. How can we be on the road to spiritual growth and sanctification if

Creative Silence

we submit so easily and so quickly to 'the snares of the devil'?

The 'encouraging word' comes from the experience of Jesus. His hour of temptation follows — if you take away the chapter heading before the fourth chapter of Matthew's Gospel — *immediately after* the most profound spiritual experience He had known, namely the descent of the Holy Spirit upon Him as He was baptised in Jordan, accompanied by the words of blessing and commendation that came from God: 'This is my beloved Son in whom I am well-pleased' (Matthew 3:17). In other words, the dedicated, consecrated life is not devoid of temptation. Indeed there may be even more of it, as the Christian life evolves. So David Watson has written in '*Is Anyone There?*' (Hodder & Stoughton): 'As soon as you find a new friend in Jesus, you make a new enemy of the devil . . . Do not be surprised, therefore, if certain things become more difficult when you have committed your life to Christ . . . Before you gave your life to Christ, Satan may not have worried much about you. Now you have become his enemy and a target for his attacks.'

It is thus confirmed from the life of Christ Himself that, as Luke notes in the Temptation story, the devil left Jesus alone 'for a season'. But he would return . . . and did; in Gethsemane: 'O my Father, if it be possible, let this cup pass from me'; on Calvary: 'My God, my God, why hast Thou forsaken me?' The same process takes place in us as good and evil wage their war in our souls. To our lives' end, we shall be tempted. The more we grow in the stature and likeness of Christ, the more will the pressures of the 'evil one' be put on us. It was the Peter who had confessed 'Thou art the Christ, the Son of the Living God' who denied Him thrice over. It was the Peter who denied Him who became the *petros*, the rock on which the church could be built. Let us not be in despair over continuing failure. Let us rather rejoice at the forgiveness that always 'makes all things new'. This is the glorious

Gospel. This is the Good News. The pattern of persistent failure is not the pattern of death. It is part of the fabric of eternal life.

The struggle within the soul has been described in many terms in the New Testament. It has been particularly expressed in the juxtaposition of the words 'flesh' and 'spirit', especially by Paul who saw the conflict in that light. These terms may not be the best terms to use today for they tend to carry sexual overtones which restrict their meaning and screen the emphasis that is essential if we are going to appreciate the real nature of the struggle in the depths. To make this into a conflict between the sexual and the spiritual would be less than just to the real nature of the conflict.

It is the word 'flesh' that is the misleading concept. 'Flesh' includes the lusts of the body, but is not confined to them. It describes in fact the whole 'worldly' attitude — that attitude that makes the material more important than the spiritual; that puts value on prestige and position; that 'leans on our own understanding'; that 'takes anxious thought for the morrow' by concentrating, not on the Kingdom of God, but on the 'other things'; that elevates the 'temporal' as important and dismisses the 'eternal' as irrelevant; that fills barns selfishly, and forgets the needs of the soul that will be 'required' at any time; that draws the map of life without the dimension of the Spirit in it.

'Flesh' is not being merely 'in the world': it is being 'of' it. It is 'savouring the things that be of men' rather than the 'things that be of God'. It is deciding 'sadly' that holding on to possessions as the rich young ruler did (Matthew 19:16–22) is more urgent than giving up all that one has and following Jesus. *All* this is 'the flesh'. All this fights against 'the spirit'. To fail to arrive at the right balance between this 'flesh' and 'spirit', does damage to our inner life. It is the aim of life to win this inner struggle. It is the Christian faith that this can only be won 'through Jesus Christ, our Lord'.

The language that speaks in words like 'flesh' and 'spirit' will sound old-fashioned to many today. It is not the language of sophisticated circles, courses on human relations, avant-garde theological circles or in academic and intellectual arguments about the problems of life. Dismiss the terms themselves, but that for which they stand remains. Life is a struggle to find the right relationship between 'positive' and 'negative', between 'false self' and 'true self', between 'lower' and 'higher' natures.

In psychological language, the same struggle can be described in terms of the gap between the good conscious part of us and the 'shadow' side of the 'unconscious' that we do not know. 'Breakdown' is always near if unconscious drives cannot be acknowledged but are further repressed. Deep in the unconscious they will ferment, ultimately to be expressed as neurotic symptoms, 'personality disorders' or even psychosomatic illness.

Integration, or in Jung's language 'individuation', comes about through the moving closer of our conscious and unconscious selves through self-awareness and self-knowledge. The personal unconscious and, even more, the 'collective unconscious' load us with burdens that are truly 'grievous and heavy to be borne'. Increasing self-awareness of what constitutes these burdens is offered as the hope that points us towards integration.

In spiritual terms, however, more is necessary than just self-awareness, however developed it is, to ensure victory in the conflict between light and darkness, good and evil, flesh and spirit. Self-awareness is but the preparation for the *gift* of the 'grace of our Lord, Jesus Christ'. Repentance is always the preliminary to 'justification' and its further expression in 'sanctification'.

We cannot repent unless we are 'self-aware', aware, that is, of the state of need which we have; aware of the cry of the heart that Paul uttered as he contemplated 'the good that he would' that was never done and 'the evil that he would not' that was expressed in action: 'Who shall deliver me from the body of this death?' His answer is the Christian answer for all time: 'I thank God, through Jesus Christ, my Lord' (Romans 7:25).

This is not mere 'God-talk', religious language without meaning or relationship to reality. It comes in fact so close to reality that to dismiss it in such terms endangers the life of the soul. The reality is (to use more religious words) 'redemption', 'salvation', 'entering the Kingdom of God', 'life everlasting', 'eternal life', etc., etc. Reality is to be 'in Christ'. We may move to more modern words if we will — 'wholeness', 'integration', 'union with the Divine', etc. What is being described by them all are the acts of God in Jesus Christ (in the Incarnation, Crucifixion and Resurrection) and in the giving of the Holy Spirit. It is only through the 'divine initiative', the taking of the first step by the God who first loves us, that the way of integration can unfold, that good can triumph over evil, that 'flesh' and 'spirit' can be brought into right relationship. That relationship is one of balance in which 'flesh' must be under the dominion of 'spirit'.

Who — or what — would control the life of Christ? This was the battle as it was fought out in the wilderness. To whom would Paul belong and whom must he serve? This was the issue faced in his silent desert. On our lesser platforms, the question is the same for us. And the answer we all return must be 'Jesus Christ, our Lord'.

*   *   *

Silence gives us the opportunity to hear what is around us in a way we have not been able to do it previously. It is not easy to hear the wind, or the birds, or the rustle of the trees in a busy city street. But in the silence of the hillside, we can hear them all. It is the same with our inner silence. When the tumult of the mind is stilled, we can become

conscious of other sounds. If the mind is at rest, soul-
voices (if I may coin such a word) will break through into
consciousness. The mind, off-duty in relation to the
pressing needs of daily life and living, can find itself aware
of quite other thoughts, intuitions, feelings as these come
into awareness. With 'earthquake, wind and fire'
receding, the 'still, small voice' can whisper its word of
illumination and the light of understanding can cross our
path.

In the previous chapter I referred to the need for
caution in reflective meditation and the inner silence
which is part of that process. That warning stands. There
are those who, for the reasons I gave, should not meditate
in this way alone. That re-emphasised, I go on to develop
the theme in relation to two points. The first is about the
contact with our inner life and being that we must seek,
and, with it, something of what the 'unconscious' means,
while the second relates to the problems that arise
through contact with the negative, shadow, 'evil' side of
our life. Engagement with our inner selves, contact with
our soul or true self does produce blessing, hope,
awareness of love and compassion, potential for service,
etc. It can also open the door to negative feelings of
anxiety and guilt and, if we are lacking in spiritual
resources, we may be disturbed by them. It is an area in
which we need to hear the words of Jesus: 'Let not your
heart be troubled: you believe in God: believe also in Me'
(John 14:1).

Is it unrealistic to make that assertion? Should we
simply ignore, or regard as unimportant these frightening
forces that threaten to upset or even overwhelm us? The
answer is, of course, 'No', and the reason for that answer
leads to another word of encouragement.

If there are feelings of failure, guilt, 'sin', as a result of
reflective meditation, then it is our responsibility to face
them. They are ours — even if cultural and heredity
factors contribute to their presence. They must be

accepted.

The alternative is to 'repress' them, to banish them from our consciousness. But this we should not do. Though we may cease to be conscious of them, they are still there in 'the unconscious', active and subtle. They will reappear, probably with renewed force. As a result we shall feel inner pressures to behave in certain ways, almost certainly irresponsible and unacceptable ways, or we shall be drawn into irritation, frustration, anger, hostility, withdrawnness. Failing all else, these repressed feelings may express themselves, as I have said, through psychosomatic illness.

I believe with all my heart, that there is no creative way to deal with our unacceptable selves or any part of us that we do not like and which we meet and recognise in the silence, other than 'face-to-face' encounter. It is in the inner silence that this can take place, for at that level the encounter can be creative.

In saying this I am saying something that does demand inner strength (hence my caution and warnings above) or, as it might be described in psychological terms, 'ego strength'. It is near to being a counsel of perfection. That does not however cancel out the demand. But it does compel me to stress that long experience of creative silence may be required to cope with the demands that come from inside us. Nevertheless it can be done, perhaps must be done, if inner peace and consequent usefulness are to be possible.

The man or woman whom God can best use is that man or woman who has seen, recognised and come to terms creatively with that secret self which the world is not allowed to see, our 'unacceptable selves'. But again the word of encouragement is repeated. Jesus faced His 'shadow' side, in the Temptation story. It was expressed in temptations as subtle and powerful as 'Satan' could contrive, for they concentrated on the one possible 'weakness' in the incarnate Christ, the temptation to abuse His divine power. It was the possibility of power (through eating of the tree of knowledge of good and evil — for 'you shall be as gods,' said the Tempter in the Garden of Eden) that brought about the fall of the 'first Adam'. It was that very area that the Tempter attacked in Christ in every way he knew (and in which he fortified himself with selective Scripture), when he sought to destroy the 'second Adam' who 'to the fight and to the rescue came'. So the divine power which Jesus would not abuse became the very power through which He could fulfil His mission of love and service.

We can apply this in some way to ourselves. In so doing we are touching the salvation of the silence for it is in the silence we find the room, the space and the power we need to deal with the inner struggle.

It is not unique or unusual to have and be aware of our unacceptable self. It is normal! Indeed the abnormal person would be the one who had no shadow side to him! 'There is none righteous, no, not one' (Romans 3:10). 'All have sinned and come short of the glory of God' (Romans 3:23). It is part of our humanity to be in this position. I recall again that even the Son of God was 'tempted like as we are'.

So we must face the reality Christians call 'sin' (not sins). If we have the courage to face it, then we must face it at its worst. The lengths to which humanity can go are awful and for each one of us personally, there is the need to say over and over again: 'There but for the grace of God, go I'. The difference between criminals and others is, largely, that criminals are caught — a humourous way of saying something which is profoundly true. The capacity of us all to engage in 'the evil which we would not' is real. The drive to 'act out' our inner feelings can become overwhelming. When such acting out takes place, the consequences can be frightening. 'From whence come wars and fighting?' asks James. 'Are they not the outward expression of that inner warfare which results from your instinctive desire for pleasure? You want something: you cannot have it: you are ready to commit murder. You passionately desire something: you are unable to get it: you fight and feud' (James 4:1–2 WB).

That is however the end of the depressing part of the story! Now triumph begins! As with the whole of life, the way to 'crown' is through 'cross': the way to resurrection is through crucifixion *and* the descent into hell. It is the demand of the silence that we accept totally our unacceptable selves. Only face-to-face encounter, I wrote above, can meet the situation creatively. We are to face, head on, our evil. Accept it and triumph begins.

Facing ourselves in the silence opens the door to a most glorious truth: it is almost certainly through the redemption of the part of ourselves we most hate and reject that we can offer most in life. Aggressiveness recognised as potential ruthlessness, self-centred and horrific, can when redeemed provide the drive that moves mountains to create that which will bless humanity. The sexual drive that, unredeemed, expresses itself in lust and even deviation or perversion can become, if recognised, faced, accepted and redeemed, the outgoing love that ministers in compassion and understanding to people in need. The survival instinct that, unredeemed, puts self first and leads to denial and betrayal, can, recognised and redeemed, become an area of growth in confidence and conviction that will make us stand up and be counted if required to do so.

It is in the silence that we come to terms both with ourselves and with God. That coming to terms can be the most creative component of our lives. It is for this reason that I speak of 'the salvation of the silence'. It is in creative silence we can go through crucifixion to resurrection, through death to life.

4

Love Resting

IT IS IN the inner silence that we begin to feel the true meaning of peace. For peace is a product of partnership with the Spirit. This we shall develop more when we come to the harvest of the Spirit. What I am concerned with now is the discovery that all make 'in the silence'. It is that the other side of activity is not inertia, but the activity of expectation. For expectation is of the essence of the silence. Without it, we shall find nothing.

In talking of the function of the mind in reflective meditation, I emphasised the need for it to set aside, for a while, the busy-ness that is its normal occupation and, *resting*, to make itself available to the conversation of the Spirit with the soul. There is no need to be anxious as to the availability of the Spirit! He is there. But it is a principle written into the rules of God's communication with men, that there must be a faith, a trustful expectancy with which the Spirit can make contact, if we are to 'receive'.

That sense of expectancy, of receptiveness, has always characterised true Christian worship and fellowship. At Pentecost, the disciples were all with one accord in one place, and ready for the ministry of the Spirit. The Sacraments are dependent on God for their efficacy for without the divine willingness to give, there is no sacramental possibility. But that laid down, the offered gift is not 'laid on' unwilling recipients. Grace is not *ex opere operato*. It must be *received*. And that means expectant faith must be present.

Sister Eva of Friedenshort has described peace as 'Love Resting'. Love is active and energetic. To love God with heart and soul and mind and strength implies effort — not the reluctant effort of unwillingness, but the enthusiastic effort of desire. But it does involve all of the heart and the strength as well as the mind and soul. To love one's neighbour involves effort and discipline. We choose our friends so loving is easier. Our 'neighbour' is not our choice and sometimes there has to be a real effort in giving in that direction. It is not human to be able to love whoever chances to be our neighbour for 'neighbours' can be difficult people! There is strain, effort and struggle in the discipline of Love.

True love in action can then be tiring and exhausting. It can also be costly. Love is a 'giving out' of energy and strength and self — and this at a price.

In every area of life, one principle holds true. We cannot 'give out' unless we 'take in'. Without the falling rain, the reservoirs go down. Without the gentle breezes, the windmill remains motionless. Without the gift of water from the sky, the rivers fail, the mountain streams dry up. Without the appropriate amount of food, strength diminishes. Without sleep, we do not have energy.

It is the same in the life of the Spirit. Unless we receive the gifts of grace, we have nothing to offer to others. Unless we drink at the well of running water, we cannot give the water of life to others. Unless we are fed with new material, we cannot offer wisdom to the world. Unless we receive new life ourselves, we cannot offer it to others. Unless we receive the love of Him who first loved us, we have no hope of finding the energy of love we are to offer to our neighbour, our brother, the world.

If therefore the giving out of love demands all the effort and energy I have suggested, there must come a time when love must rest and 'take in'. Peace is love resting. It is love resting in order to be renewed. The renewal takes place in the inner silence.

Let us look at this kind of peace.

Peace is first a time of 'non-activity'. It is a reducing down, even a switching-off of the active, energetic, demanding process of love-giving. 'The Apostles returned to Jesus and told Him all about what they had done and taught. "Come away by yourselves into a *lonely* place," He said, "come and *rest* for a little while"' (Mark 6:30–31 WB).

It is necessary to rest, difficult as it is to do it. There is, moreover, no rest that is as difficult to create as the mind at rest. We can lay the body down, and we can even fall asleep, but the mind is not stilled. We toss and heave 'restlessly', beseeching our troubled minds to be at peace, and they will not. We sleep officially, but we do not rest. In dreams and nightmares, our agitated minds — and behind them our rest-less souls — make their presence felt in anxiety and inner tumult.

Yet if we are to return to the service of love, that rest must come. The peace of love resting must be found. If it does not happen, if there is no blessedness of rest, how can we love tomorrow with *all* our mind and heart and soul and strength? The tumult of the winds and waves of anxiety must be stilled by One who says 'Peace, be still!' So 'the winds ceased and there was a great calm' (Matthew 8:27).

But such resting does not equal inertia, apathy, mental or soulful sloth. It is a new kind of activity. Resting means receptiveness — a readiness to receive where the mood is, paradoxically, not passive but active. It is the activity of expectation. It is the attentive waiting of the ready heart. Here activity is the right kind of activity. It is the activity appropriate to the silence. It is creative activity in the creative silence.

Peace is, secondly, the profound feeling of security that comes from the resolution of the struggle within. We go back to that inner battle I have described and the necessity of accepting our 'unacceptable selves'. The ability to face and accept all that we are and pass it over to the God who has never done other than accept us at that level brings all the peace — and joy — that Paul found in resolution of his own spiritual dilemma. The awful struggle to deny his true nature was over. No more did he believe he had to obey the law perfectly to please God. No longer must he deny the 'law in his members' that showed itself in doing the evil he would not and failing to produce the good he wanted to show. 'The strife is o'er, the battle won.' Salvation was a gift, not a ghastly fight with self with no hope of victory. 'Who shall deliver me from this death? I thank God through Jesus Christ, my Lord.'

In the desert, in the silence we see things as they are. No longer need we preserve the masks, or act our parts. We are face to face with reality. The silence we observe externally does then become also the inner silence where the miracle of grace takes place. Here do we 'touch and handle things unseen'. Here are we stripped of every outward garment hiding our true selves. Here we can embrace the awfulness of our human condition and the awesomeness of the offered gift of grace. Here the silence that may have spoken to us of sadness because of our sin now resounds with the gladness of sin forgiven. We are in touch at last with reality — our human reality and the divine reality meeting, our false self redeemed to become true, our weakness taken into the strong divine embrace.

There is no need to fear the desert; no need, if we are supported by the community of grace, to dread the silence; no need to stand back from the acknowledgement of self because we despise that self. To accept and offer ourselves, 'warts and all', is to find doors opened to new opportunity, parts of ourselves redeemed for glorious service, integration. And it is all through the Spirit.

Be still . . .

The Spirit seeks us out in love . . .

Our faith, our expectation enables that Spirit to enter . . .

There is meeting in the silence . . .

And only one possible end . . .

Life is made new . . .

We are on the way to wholeness . . .

Integration is taking place . . .

Through the Spirit.

5

The Way of Meditation

'WHEN YOU SAY your prayers, go into your private room and shut your door . . .' So Jesus put it (as William Barclay translates St. Matthew's Gospel). It is the same with the other ways to the inner silence — meditation, contemplation, etc. Personal meditation — if that can safely be undertaken — needs private space and peace.

This is equally true for the complementary road (it is that rather than an alternative road) to the inner silence, the way of the meditation group. Both are important. The Christian faith is, as I have said, both 'personal' and 'community', and this is reflected in the meditation processes. Where two or three are gathered together 'in My Name', there is even greater potential than that available when each meditates on his or her own.

In this chapter I want to say some practical things about meditation, using that word entirely in the context of the creative silence I have been discussing in this book. I am not, for example, describing a technique like Transcendental Meditation, so much advertised these days. TM (as it is widely known) is primarily a set of techniques, evolved to reduce strain and stress, encourage relaxation and create, through such a relaxation process, a better co-ordinated body and a more relaxed mind. Its protagonists make clear that it is not a religious exercise, though some individuals who use it do, no doubt, relate it to the religious life. It is a method of body–mind relaxation designed to improve physical and mental processes and it has value for some in that context. The cautionary note I have already emphasised on the possible dangers of meditation processes holds good here.

The value of TM and similar methods can be scientifically measured and shown by bio-feedback methods (for example in the work of Dr. Maxwell Cade). My concern here is with a discipline for the devotional life in relation to growth in the spiritual dimension of our being. This is the 'integration through the Spirit' which is the wholeness we need and seek today. It is not an 'other-worldly' process, nor an 'escape from reality'. It is an encounter with Reality that results in service in this world of the most practical kind possible. Indeed, if service and care do not result from meditation, the whole process should be questioned. Inner silence is creative silence.

No-one has walked closer to God than did our Lord. He demonstrates the nature of the relationship between inner silence and service in the world. 'I and my Father are one,' He said of His relationship to God. 'The man who loves God must love His neighbour,' He said of service to man.

So far I have said that the essential attitude of meditation is *relaxed attention*. This apparently paradoxical requirement is, in fact, made up of two elements that are both essential to finding the creative silence.

First we must 'be still'. The stillness is in itself a form of relaxation. Our normal state for the living of life is one of 'tension'. Our senses, muscles, nervous systems, are 'at the ready' in order that we may survive. Survival, defensive and creative action demand tension. It is like the plane at the end of the runway, waiting to take off. The engines are 'revved up', ready to go into action, but the brakes are still on. Release the brakes and all is 'go'! When we turn, however, to the needs of the soul, all that tension has to be relaxed and a stillness allowed to take over. At this point, whether it be alone or in your meditation group, 'go into your private room and shut the door'.

Relaxation is not apathy. It is not sagging into a chair and reclining sloppily. It is stillness with a view to attention, to waiting on God, to receptiveness and the heightened spiritual awareness that brings. It is desirable then to sit firmly on a chair, preferably one that encourages a straight back, with feet comfortably placed and apart (legs should not be crossed). The hands may lie conveniently in the lap, though some may want to hold them open, palms upwards (a symbolic expression of receptiveness). The aim of the physical posture is to do everything possible to create *relaxed attention*.

Let us now go back to what I have already said on the function of the mind in the meditation process. The mind has the task of ensuring we stay alive and cope with all the demands that life in a complex world creates. This is a full-time job! It certainly is the *normal* work on which our minds are engaged. But in meditation, the mind must turn from that 'daily round and common task' to its other important function. It has to give up, meantime, the servicing of the daily work of the body in order to undertake the sublime task of service to the soul. Then the stilling of the mind in relaxed attention becomes possible — and safe, for you dare not do this in a busy street — because, in our private room, with door shut, we are safe and secure from external threat. All our attention can now be turned in the direction of the soul.

The stilled mind is the gateway to contact with the things of the Spirit mediated through that part of us that is given to us for spiritual purposes, the soul.

The hardest part of meditation is the discovery of the ability to still the mind. For that reason, meditation must be gradually learned. In the early stages, words are more necessary than later on when they cease to play such an important part. Long silences are acceptable only after much experience of the ability to accept and rejoice in silence without and within. What are also found to be essential in the earlier stages of meditation, are means to focus the attention and so prevent the work and business of the world constantly entering into the silence. A multitude of thoughts are liable to invade our attempted silences — things we have to do, things we have not done, the tasks of tomorrow, the children's needs, and all the associated ideas that compete for attention, plus, inevitably, the anxieties and worries, the frustrations and fears that impinge on our consciousness from the unconscious.

We do, therefore, need a focus within our meditation period, so that concentration on that one point (we shall look, in a moment, at the possibilities) will occupy the whole of our attention and lead us into a silence that is creative and productive. And when our mind 'wanders' (and who, in meditation or at prayer does not know this problem all too well?), there is that focal point to which one can be drawn back.

In the various fields of meditation in vogue today many ways are used to focus attention ... mantras (the repetition of a particular word, phrase or sound), fantasy journeys, guided fantasy, etc., etc. My concern is solely with aids to worship, means to develop the devotional life, food to nurture the soul, integration through the Spirit, and I simply point towards ways to which I am used, to fulfil that aim.

* * *

The focus in meditation may be an idea, an image, a significant phrase, a spiritually profound theme, an object or a combination of any of these suggestions. In the early stages of the discipline, it may be more necessary to use frequent sentences or words appropriate to the theme to break up the silences. Later, words will become less necessary and silences will be much longer. Two or three phrases are all that are needed in developed meditation situations and even these might, in due course, reduce down to nothing more than an introductory sentence, with up to 45 minutes of silence following.

The leader will have a sensitivity to the silence which

will protect those who long for such silence and help those for whom too much silence is threatening.

The 'fundamentals' of life are pregnant with possibilities in meditation terms. *Water* provides a theme of the utmost profundity, associated as it is with life itself (we cannot live without it), with cleansing (and so forgiveness), with baptism (and so new life), with (in terms of John's Gospel) wine and therefore sacramental blessing. Phrases like 'living water' (from the story of the woman of Samaria with whom Jesus held such an important conversation) and 'the water of life' will have their own impact in the silence. *Air* leads us easily to 'wind' and 'breath' and directly to the Spirit, for we have those direct links made for us by Jesus Himself as well as by the story of the First Pentecost and the Spirit's coming being associated with a 'rushing, mighty wind'. *Fire* leads us quickly to devotional depths. 'Tongues of fire' herald the Spirit's presence as did a bush on fire for Moses.

For those far developed in meditative terms, the mere mention of (say) 'wings' will be enough. They will take flight on the wings of the Spirit (for the Spirit descended onto Christ in the form of a dove), and the soul will be lifted up thereby. But for those less used to meditation, the theme of 'wings' could provide a series of focal points that would maintain attention over quite a long period. There are examples of meditations set out in the Appendix to this book. Here I simply indicate the areas into which meditating on, for example, the theme of 'wings', might take us (the Meditation is given in full in the Appendix):

Inspiration: they that wait upon the Lord shall mount up with wings . . .

Providence: in the shadow of Thy wings will I make my refuge.

Compassion: how often would I have gathered thy children together, even as a hen gathereth her chickens under her wings . . .

Healing: the Sun of Righteousness will arise with healing in his wings.

For some a symbol such as a rose or a tree will lead into the deep places. (For a helpful illustrated meditation on a tree, see the Community of the Resurrection series from Mirfield, West Yorkshire, England). A tree has roots, reaches upwards, draws on the elements of sun, wind and rain, spreads out in shelter and protection. The tree of life has leaves that are 'for the healing of the nations' (see Revelation 22 for this reference and so much helpful symbolism of this kind).

A passage that can be used for meditation in either of these forms is Luke 1:76–79. It is full of profound phrases written round 'the day-spring from on high' (see Appendix). For another passage of extraordinary profundity and potential nurture, try Ephesians 3:14 to the end of the chapter, particularly in the *New English Bible* version.

But there are no rigid rules and no real limitations. What is meditatively helpful to *you* is valid. The pace is *yours*. The aim of all of it is to touch the deeper levels of spiritual awareness, so largely untapped in our kind of world, and through that to move towards wholeness in Christ. At Christmas you will simply want, in meditation, to follow the star and find through it, as wise men of old did, that the Lord is to be found; that in the pure and holy Mary, there is a richness that enriches every life; that we may sit with shepherds on some hillside and 'see the angels' with child-like faith: that the extraordinary self-giving of Joseph lay in his own deeply spiritual intuition and that all he did played a part in making it possible for the holy child of Bethlehem to be 'ours today'.

At Palm Sunday time, in meditation we can join with the crowds who spread their garments in the way of the lord of life. In the eventide of life, it will be possible to empathise with Simeon and go on our journey in peace because 'our eyes have seen Thy salvation'.

There is no fixed route to salvation and the health of the soul ... though so many try to confine the Spirit by insisting that there is.

What matters is that we find the way that leads to life. If meditation helps anyone to draw on the waters of eternity or feel the winds of the Spirit, it is then a gift, truly given. Used properly and profoundly, with responsibility and true abandon, it can make open a way to the creative inner silence.

6

The Development of the Life of the Spirit

THE INNER SILENCE that is a creative silence, is the basis of the cultivation of that deep centre within us that, in the end, brings true balance. We cannot grow towards real health or wholeness if we neglect the growth of the spiritual part of our being, for we are *spiritual* beings. Any philosophy of life that fails to acknowledge this truth is, in the words of the old evangelical hymn, a 'broken cistern'. 'We've tried the broken cisterns, Lord, but ah! the waters failed. . . . There's none but Christ can satisfy . . .'. So the old hymn puts it.

This is indeed old-fashioned evangelical language and, as such, will cut little ice today, but the oddity (if it may be felt to be such) of the language does not deny the truth of the statement itself. Mankind continues to put its trust in all kinds of 'broken cisterns' and, despite repeated failure to find satisfaction, persists in pursuing philosophies that must fall short of 'satisfaction' because they deny or play down the spiritual dimension. So the list of modern heresies grows ever longer. Stars followed with eagerness and enthusiasm have failed to provide salvation. The belief that, first science, then education, then psychology would provide the whole answer to man's deepest needs, lies crushed, battered. The false pursuits go on: the Christian remedy remains — as relevant today as yesterday, as relevant tomorrow, as relevant for ever.

However it is to be expressed, in sophisticated contemporary concepts or in simple evangelical songs, 'there's none but Christ that satisfies, there is no other name for me!' The redemption of life, the salvation of the soul, the attainment of wholeness, individuation, integration — call it what you will — involves Christ at the centre and integration through the Spirit. This is the truth about life.

The development of the spiritual life through the inner silence must not be thought to be an emphasis on the individualistic side of faith, an emphasis which is out of balance with mature Christianity. The Christian Faith is, as I have said, both individual, personal *and* communal, and no separation of these two concepts dare be made. Loving God and loving our neighbour are inescapably linked and no true balance can be achieved in Christian living where one half of this whole is under-emphasised. The development of the spiritual life and emphasis on the spiritual dimension are as important for balance in community health and growth as they are for individual welfare.

It is this that brings the spiritual dimension into the practical life of the world. An educational approach that ignores spiritual growth and development fails at the most crucial point. A political programme that takes no account of the essentially spiritual nature of man cannot ultimately minister to the people's good. A national health service that refuses to go beyond the boundaries and limitations of 'orthodox' medicine denies the reality of the other areas of man's being. So the man or woman who nourishes the soul does not become less involved with the life of the world, but can only become more concerned, with compassion and creativity. To apply our hearts and minds to whatever can help develop the spiritual life is far from engaging in irrelevance or escapism. It is probably, on the contrary, a supremely important task, and a relevant one.

But the Spirit has a language of His own . . .

*   *   *

Karl Rahner, in *Meditations on Freedom and the Spirit*, talks about those 'unavoidable words which open up the mysterious totality of human existence'. He is referring, of course, to a group of words that are not 'clear and precise', like the nouns which can be 'clarified and classified' 'precisely and scientifically'. Though 'not similarly clear and precise' the 'unavoidable words . . . cannot be denied meaning and validity. They are words which relate specifically to human life, which are concerned with man as a whole . . . man where spirit and freedom are constantly stretching out beyond the trivial and limited nature of the finite reality within his empirical experience, until finally he is lost in that mysterious darkness which embraces and enfolds all human existence.'

The linguistic distinction Rahner makes is valuable when we consider the point Jesus made in His exposition of the meaning of being 'in' or 'of' the world (see, especially, John 17). These two prepositions imply an enormous distinction in the values and attitudes, the words and thoughts appropriate to the stand we take. If we are 'in' the world, we shall use one set of concepts, one kind of language, one corpus of values and attitudes. If we are 'in' it, but not 'of' it, we shall look for another language, different concepts, and other values and attitudes. Our whole perspective about life will be different. The problem, both at a personal level and at the level of relationship, is to keep lines of communication open between the two very different philosophies of life that each stance implies. Perhaps those lines of communication can only be kept open through those who, to go back to Tillich's phrase, are 'living on the boundary'.

The problem is a particular one for products of a scientific background . . . which means it is a problem for many today. We have been raised in a world governed by the scientific point of view. We have been conditioned by the materialism which is directly related to scientifically and technologically conditioned people. The scientist has authority because he deals with the 'real' and the 'proved'. The doctor has authority because of the scientific nature and sophistication of his profession. All other healing processes are suspect, unacceptable to his professional association.

Even deeply spiritual people find it hard to step outside the scientific, the medical and the materialistic approaches. Young people who reject materialism are 'odd', 'hippy', 'immature', 'irresponsible'. The norms and the definitions of responsibility relate to the material world we know so well, and by which we are conditioned.

All this makes it very difficult for the language of the Spirit and soul to carry any 'ring of truth' to scientifically conditioned people and even more so to materially conscious people. It is, as it were, the language of another world. And if, perchance, there are those who acknowledge the possibility of such language, but relegate it to Sunday worship where it stays outwardly respected, though inwardly rejected, the problems grow even greater. The rejection of the language of the Spirit and the soul as irrelevant, ineffective and unworldly by so many church-people, has driven young people who seek for this dimension to look for it outside the churches.

Such a development is tragic. At the very time in history that mankind is beginning to learn that 'man does not live by bread alone', the churches have been found wanting, not because of their unwillingness, their hostility or their ineffectiveness but because they have 'lost their treasure'.

This is, of course, wide generalisation, but it is valid comment, too. It is not a criticism of others only, it is self-criticism. That said, it leaves us all with a real problem. We cannot offer the spiritual depths to others until we rediscover them ourselves. It is to do this I have outlined the meaning of creative silence. It is through the inner silence we come into touch with the Spirit, speaking to our souls. It is through the contact of soul with Spirit, we grow in grace.

Let us turn, then, to the tools of that growth out of

which, ultimately, the harvest of the Spirit comes.
These tools are 'the means of grace'.

7

Means of Grace

'THE MEANS OF GRACE' refer to everything provided by God to enable grace to 'flow' into us as His gift. They include worship, prayer, the sacraments, meditation, the community and fellowship — the koinonia — of the church, laying on of hands, etc. It is not my purpose in this short devotional study to deal comprehensively with all the means of grace — or indeed with every one of them. But a brief comment may be helpful on some of them and I turn first to the concept of the church in relation to the means of grace.

So many attitudes to the church are conditioned by misunderstandings about the nature of 'the church'. Most of the criticism of 'the church' is criticism of the institutional expression of 'the church' or of its representatives. It is crucial to remember (I know this is the statement of the obvious, but it is often forgotten at practical levels) that 'the church' is always *people*, not stones or institutions. It is the *con-gregation* of people who 'have one faith and serve one Lord'. It is the *ekklesia*, the *elect*, those 'called out'; not elect to damnation or salvation (as has been the emphasis put on the concept of 'election' in some theological systems) but called out and chosen for a purpose, namely to serve.

Election to service is the privilege and responsibility put on those whom God calls. The privilege is given not because they are 'better than other men are' — indeed it compels a humility born of the honour of 'chosen-ness'. The chosen, the called are rooted 'in the world' but they are not 'of' it. They are one with mankind, but 'separate' from 'the world'. Their responsibilities are special because they have been accorded the privilege of election to service. The church is *people*, people called together to be the people of God and with all the responsibilities such election requires, an election always to be demonstrated in humility and never in self-righteousness or spiritual arrogance.

It is a means of grace to be part of the body of Christ. For that reason those of us who take a sacramental view of the baptism of infants see such a step as important. It is a central tenet of almost all modern conceptual systems in psychology with its various theories of child development, that the influences by which a child is surrounded, from the first moments of time (and some today would push it even further back than that, into the pre-birth condition), influence that child, *though it is not cognitively conscious of or able to remember in the normal sense of memory, either the influences that surround it or the lack of such influences.* While we do not consciously remember that which impinges on us in these babyhood years, nevertheless those influences are recorded in our 'unconscious' selves, and become part of us. *Is it not then important, that, from the earliest moments in our lives, we should be within the climate of grace and so be in touch with the dimension of the holy, even though we are not conscious of it?*

Those who say they can live the life of grace and be in touch with God without ever going to a church may be expressing something valid, but, remembering the relationship of individual faith and community responsibility (in other words the call to love God and our neighbour), dare we stand outside 'the people of God', 'the church', 'the body of Christ' — indeed the whole climate of grace? We are closing the door to an essential element of grace in the development of our spiritual life if we do. At the same time we are asking for the benefits of faith while setting aside its responsibilities. 'There is no need for me to belong to the church, for I can worship God as effectively on the hills' is so often said. We can — and many do — worship God on hills, in woods and by the water, but the other side of Christian privilege and responsibility is omitted. The product of worship is service. The result of accepting the invitation to 'Come unto Me' is a willingness to 'go into all the world'.

Faith and service, grace-full receiving and obedience, faith and 'following' are inseparable. Buildings are not essential to the life of faith and grace, but participation in the responsibilities of the Kingdom is. To receive the gift of grace is to feel the desire to make it available to others. To be 'justified' must lead to 'sanctification' for self and others. Conversion must lead to concern. To feel the love of God who 'first loved us' is to be compelled to love our neighbour, for there is an 'eternal triangle' of love at the heart of the Gospel — the love of God for us — and our neighbour, the love we owe to God — and our neighbour owes to God — and to us. Worship without service leads (as I said earlier) to the establishment of a pious club, but not 'the church'. The church always lives 'in' the world though it is not 'of' it. Christians, just because they are in a restored 'right relationship' to Christ feel the more the call to serve the world in love.

So the church is essentially neither buildings nor institution. It is Christ's people, having one faith, serving one Lord, scattered (like salt) in the world, creating a climate of grace, and taking on the responsibility to make humanity aware that life abundant, true life, takes in the spiritual dimension without which no one can be 'in their true element'. Participation in the life of the church is a means of grace through which spiritual development, born in the inner silence where Christ, through the Spirit, meets with the soul, is nurtured — or should be. To be within the climate of grace, the environment of the holy, is to be within areas of spiritual influence. These will affect us whether we know it or not. So in our seeking whatever helps us in ministering to our inner being, stress must be put on membership of and participation in the community of grace, Christ's people, the church. *There* we are, I repeat, within the climate of grace. From there we can contribute to creating the climate of grace for the blessing of others.

*   *   *

It is hard to believe that there is a means of grace more moving and sanctifying than the Sacrament of the Lord's Supper. Here indeed we do (as I have already quoted) 'touch and handle things unseen' and in so doing bring ourselves within the reach of new sources of grace. Can it be possible to be within sight and sound of this Sacrament and not experience something of the climate of grace to which it contributes? As the centurion at the Cross was forced to proclaim some kind of divinity emanating from the crucified prophet he did not know but whose divine presence he felt, so the heart will cry out, in participating in the Sacrament, that the divine presence is truly here, 'in the midst'. 'The bread and wine remove, but Thou art here . . . . Nearer than ever . . .'

The Lord's Supper is important in its ability to nurture the soul. I see it as imperative that our view of the Sacrament is one that does not in any way diminish either its significance or its 'sealing' capacity. It is an occasion when we remember but it is also an occasion when we receive. The Sacrament is a medium (or means) of grace. It is not just a sign or a symbol. The occasion is *sacramental*. In the Sacrament, given that there is receptive faith, *God acts*.

Some of the most spiritually creative groups in the Christian community do not, of course, put any importance on 'internal' means of grace such as the sacraments. The Quakers (Society of Friends) and the Salvation Army are two examples of outstanding Christian bodies or churches, but they do not celebrate the Lord's Supper as most main-stream churches do, yet both manifestly create a climate of grace. I stress therefore that the Dominical Sacraments (the two sacraments of Baptism and Communion instituted on our Lord's authority as the position is seen in, for example, my own tradition — Church of Scotland) are not the *only* means of grace. They are nevertheless outstandingly 'grace-conveying' occasions and I stress their importance as such in the growth and development of the spiritual life. Deep in the soul, where lie the yearnings of the spiritual explorer and the longing for reconciliation, reunion and true peace, the sacramental touch graciously forwards the sanctifying process — another tiny area redeemed, another insight revealed, another step along the path initiated. The 'validity' of the Sacraments, their ability to convey grace, is of course not established by us. That comes from the nature of their institution (by our Lord), our use of the appointed symbols and our faith that Christ is present and active in the sacraments. All these factors present, grace is there to be received.

In the Sacrament of the Lord's Supper, Christ alone is the Celebrant, making the occasion not just a memorial feast but making it a symbol, sign and seal of God's grace upon us and within us. And this is a communal as well as an individual happening, for it takes place within the community of grace that radiates outwards a climate of grace, or should.

The Sacrament is a 'mystery' — and a mystery that is only comprehensible from within the faith. To the unbeliever, this is only an empty rite, puzzling and even offensive, but to those who believe in God through Christ in the Spirit, this means of grace will 'feed' the conscious mind and the unconscious being with 'the grace of our Lord Jesus Christ'. This is indeed a means of grace that will help us grow in the likeness of Christ.

* * *

Prayer is, obviously, a means of grace of enormous importance in the development of the spiritual man or woman. The discipline of prayer is an essential part of spiritual growth. None can afford to neglect this means of grace.

It is not my purpose here to write a manual on prayer — there are many others who have done this with authority and skill. I content myself with saying that prayer is not a sequence of acts so much as a state in which we are called to live. It is life lived out in the presence of God. It is not so much words as relationship. It is not so much a set of actions, however liturgically splendid, as much as it is the practice of the presence of God. It is the living out of a relationship with the Divine in the hard realities of this earthly life.

Prayer is not a matter of speaking. It is that, but it is also a pattern of listening. As with any human relationship, there cannot be monologue without threatening the relationship entirely. Prayer is two-way relationship that includes both speaking and listening. There is no doubt who is the dominant partner in the relationship for it is the Divine initiative in relationship that enables us to be in touch with God, but it is real relationship — and that means understanding, empathy, sympathy and sensitivity. All these are the marks of good relationship.

The point I make about listening is important if we are seriously concerned with spiritual development. Elijah, in his period of crisis, had to learn that God was not always in the dramatic and the extraordinary, but could be found by listening to the still, small voice. Silence in prayer is an important aspect of the relationship that brings grace and growth.

Prayer is not the same as meditation. There is a certain balance towards the 'active' side in prayer just as there is a certain 'passivity' — or something like it — in meditation. But the habit of meditation will deepen and enrich the practice of prayer, for the very communion of soul with Spirit in creative silence will bring new wonder into adoration, new depth into confession, new understanding into supplication and new breadth into intercession. The relationship of prayer will be enriched by the deepened awareness of 'the holy' that meditation brings.

'Let us pray' is not a formal call to those who come to church. It is the call to explore the divine relationship anew each time and, out of that relationship, with its intimacy of spoken and unspoken word, a capacity for growth in the spiritual life will come.

Prayer is truly a means of grace.

8

The Grace-full Man

TO MAKE a person into a means would normally be indefensible but to make a man or a woman into a 'means of grace' that will take us further along the road to a grace-full life is to do them honour. Grace comes through people, too.

It was asked of that great Scottish churchman, Dr. John White of 'The Barony' in Glasgow, just where he found the spiritual resources that made him the Christian that he was. He replied simply: 'I met a Man'. Meeting the grace-full man, woman or child is always a grace-full experience. Whether it be an encounter by voice alone with someone at a distance, or a close encounter of a fleeting kind with someone on the path, a loving relationship with someone of like mind or heart, the intimate and profound meeting of souls across the years or the life-long companionship with another — each will offer examples of the medium, the means, of grace that has brought blessing. I met a man. I met a woman. I met . . .

What are the characteristics of this grace-full man or woman?

In older times this might well have taken us into a discussion of the 'morals' of the Christian man or woman, but that word and the sort of concepts it brings forward are not synonymous with 'grace'. The moral man is not always the grace-full man — as St. Paul would be quick to confirm. Saul of Tarsus was a *very* moral man *before* he became Paul. He had a moral pedigree as impressive as his religious and national status. But he was not a man full of grace. The Pharisees observed moral rules, but how far short of all we now see — through Christ — as grace-full, they were! There was little grace in the kind of religion they proclaimed. The 'rich young ruler' had kept all the commandments 'from his youth up', but sadly was unable to accept the real standard of a Christian disciple, the readiness to give up everything for Christ's sake.

Simon the Pharisee, Jesus' dinner host, felt the weight of Jesus' rebuke for his technical but grace-less righteousness and commended the tears of the sincerely loving, though technically sinning, woman of 'bad reputation' who washed His feet with her tears.

Many with orthodox ecclesiastical attitudes need to consider this juxtaposition very seriously. True religion, true grace-fullness is bound up with concepts like leaving all, giving all, launching out into the deep and going out not knowing where we are going, much more than the rigidities of religious regulations or the securities, personal or financial, that are stressed in so much contemporary thinking.

I am therefore concerned here, not to expound technical morality (though we would all benefit from more morality at national and international as well as personal levels), but to touch the true qualities and values of the grace-full disciple.

There is no doubt as to what the most fundamental quality of the grace-full man is. It is humility. It is not without real significance that Jesus, hearing the disciples discussing who would be greatest in the Kingdom 'called a little child to Him, and set him in the midst of them and said: "Except ye be converted, and become as little children, you cannot enter the Kingdom of Heaven"' (Matthew 18:2–4).

A profound humility (I need not stress that this is a world away from 'humbleness' of the worldly kind) is a mark of the most grace-full man of all, Jesus Christ. Paul saw clearly the meaning and significance of that life of profound humility and created one of the greatest passages in the New Testament as he stressed the need for Christians to have 'the mind which was also in Christ

Jesus' (Philippians 2:5–11 WB).

> He shared the very being of God, but He did
> not regard His equality with God as a thing to
> be clutched to Himself. So far from that, He
> emptied Himself and really and truly became a
> servant, and was made for a time exactly like
> men. In a human form that all could see, He
> accepted such a depth of humiliation that He
> was prepared to die, and to die on a cross. That
> is why God has given Him the name that is
> greater than any name, so that at the name of
> Jesus every creature in heaven, and on earth
> and beneath the earth should kneel in
> reverence and submission, and so that
> everything which has a voice should openly
> declare that Jesus Christ is Lord, and thus bring
> glory to God the Father.

Much has been made down the centuries of the
emanations of energy radiating from all living things. So
far as human beings are concerned, esoteric, psychic and
spiritual circles have, with varying emphases, talked and
written of the aura that surrounds us all. The halo is, in
symbolic form, the 'reality' that is visible to 'spiritual
eyes'. Now that the things familiar to sages and seers are
entering the realms of science, much experimentation and
exploration is going on in this whole area of energy
emanation. Diagnostic use of the aura, long dismissed as
superstition or psychic oddity or as the illusions of
metaphysicians and the exaggeration of esoterics, now
moves into the region of the acceptable.

The point I make from this digression is the reality of
the felt presence of people — for good or ill. Put it in
whatever terms you like, it is part of our experience that
we feel ill at ease in the nearer presence of some people,
for reasons we cannot put into words and find it
impossible to understand. It is equally true that, without

our being able to explain it, the presence of others is restful, peaceful, inspiring and comforting. 'Come unto Me, all ye that labour and are heavy-laden, and I will give you rest . . . you shall find rest unto your souls' (Matthew 11:28–30). 'He came sweet influence to impart, a gracious, willing guest' (Harriet Auber). The Holy Spirit is the radiating influence promised by 'our blest Redeemer'. So the grace-full man or woman gives forth such a radiance, though he does not know it and she cannot understand it. It is a product of the indwelling of the Holy Spirit. It cannot be consciously or deliberately created. It cannot be acquired by effort or money (what a ghastly mis-understanding of this principle was shown by Simon in Acts, Chapter 8). It is, in fact, the effort to acquire that so often prevents acquisition. Such radiance is a gift of grace alone. Only because it is a gift can it become a means of grace, a medium of grace to others.

The community of grace, radiating a climate of grace is — or ought to be — composed of grace-full men and women through whose very presence we are made whole. To be such a means of grace to others is indeed a privilege that moves to humility. To receive, through this personal 'means' of grace, is to feel in the presence of a gift, the gift of the Holy Spirit through Jesus Christ, our Lord.

* * *

'I met a man.' The search for the clue to the development of the spiritual life, born in the silent encounter between soul and Spirit, constantly takes us back to one vantage point — a looking unto Jesus. It is on the mystery of the Incarnation that the disciple must ponder as he or she seeks the pattern of grace-full living. We have seen that the mark of the Master is His humility and *that* we must endeavour to make part of us. For it is the One who was 'God of God . . . and was made man' (as the Nicene Creed expresses it) in whom we see the basis of the 'holy worldliness' that is the mark of God's people. The 'one Lord Jesus Christ, the only begotten Son of God ... very God of very God ... who for us men and for our salvation, came down from Heaven and was incarnate by the Holy Ghost of the Virgin Mary' is that unique person we cannot emulate, but the emphasis He embodies points to the nature of our own pattern for living. We are human, in every respect, yet called to be, by grace alone, sons of God. We are earth of the earth and yet we have here 'no abiding city.' We are 'in' the world but not to be 'of' it. Our priority is the search for the Kingdom of Heaven, leaving the other things to be added in proper proportion. We must see 'the things that are seen' as nothing more than temporal because the things that are eternal are our real concern. So we are called to an inter-twining, in an inter-relationship of mystery, of the humanity we truly have and the divinity to which we are called, a divinity which is a gift of grace as well as a reality of humble experience. True, we only see through a glass darkly, while our touching of the divine is only an inkling of the reality that is to be, but of the reality, we have, in fleeting moments of heightened awareness, intuitional experience that is confirmed objectively in the records of the saints.

The 'holy worldliness' to which we are called is a life lived out in the world against the background of the 'inklings of eternity' (as J B Phillips names them) in our experience. To worldliness we can never be summoned, but to 'holy' worldliness we are. The content of that word 'holy' is therefore relevant in relation to our spiritual growth.

Holy worldliness involves both distance and involvement. The 'worldliness' is the involvement. 'Holiness' is the distance. It is part of our humanity, our being human, to be wholly caught up in the life of the world ... in the sense in which William Temple said that Christianity is the most materialistic of all religions. We are in the world, sharing its joy, pain and suffering, endeavouring to feel and help to solve its problems, empathising through our common humanity with the height, depth, breadth and length of the human condition. But we are not 'of' the world. There has to be a 'set-apartness', a distance that is of the essence of holiness, for holiness is essentially about 'setting apart'. Indeed these are words much associated with the implications of ordination. Our Lord was 'like as we are', truly human, but He was also divine, and to that extent 'apart' from the world.

Given much of the thinking dominant in churches this half-century, I feel less need to dwell on the 'worldliness' than on the 'holy'. Through the fifties, and to some extent, the sixties, we heard much of the concept of the 'servant church', called to identify itself with humanity, called to serve humanity. That emphasis persists . . . and rightly so. Christianity *is* the most materialistic of all religions. But I am concerned about the 'holy' aspect. It is noticeable that in our times the true and proper apartness of the priest has been endangered by the apparent pressure many religious and clergy feel to be 'as other men (and women) are', to use (but even more so) the language of the world, to risk the loss of a proper apartness by familiarity and intimacy of such a kind that there is no clear distinction left between being *in* but not *of* the world.

The recovery of apartness — and, in that sense, holiness — must be a discipline for all who seek sanctification or, in more contemporary terms, growth in the inner life. It is not an exercise in morals (as I said earlier), for morality as such is not the centre of the spiritual quest. It is the discovery of the right kind of balance, a balance based on the priority of the spiritual dimension in life. Out of that kind of balance, goodness will come — as we shall see in our later chapters on 'The Harvest of the Spirit'.

Life in the world puts subtle pressures upon us. The

simple faith, holy innocence and sense of wonder of 'the child in the midst' are so easily diminished — and can be totally destroyed — by the sophistication of the kind of society that we face today. The philosophies of our time extol the logical and the rational. The achievements of our time enhance the stature of science and technology. The pressures of social conformity make us less independent in our judgements and less trustingly intuitive in our apprehension of the deeper things. The hidden persuaders cry affluence, not poverty. The modern traders in the destruction of the body as the Temple of the Spirit cry 'licence' and 'freedom', not chastity. The standards of acceptance in the world put a premium on prestige rather than humility. It is too easy to *con*-form to the standards of the world when it is *trans*-forming grace that is the true road to rich life.

It is not the Christian's responsibility to opt out of 'the world'. As it was for our Lord Himself, so we are placed, feet on the ground, within it. It is however, the Christian's responsibility to realise the call to 'holiness' and accept the true apartness this involves, an apartness possible through the sanctified life of the soul through the Spirit. The offering of holy worldliness can be our gift and blessing to the world and make us truly a personal means of grace.

*   *   *

Let us look, finally, in this section on the nurture of the spiritual life at four elements that I see as playing a part in the make-up of the grace-full man or woman. These all enable such people to minister more fully as true means of grace. They are qualities needed in facing the stormy waters of life triumphantly, but they are all infectious qualities that radiate outwards towards others and so contribute to another's growth in grace. They have all been mentioned earlier, but I add a particular word on them now.

The first is *balance*. Though I have spoken of this concept already, I make no apology for returning to it. I believe it to be a key word in creative living.

Life is best when we strike the right balance between 'heart, soul, mind and strength'; between 'physical, emotional, mental and spiritual' in relation to the Spirit and the Spiritual.

Jesus was the wholly balanced man. There was a proper inter-dependence between body, mind, heart (or the emotions) and soul/spirit but all was (as it were) encompassed by the presence and indeed centrality of the power of the Holy Spirit. So everything our Lord said and did was witness to balance. In that He was the perfect man. 'The disciple must be as His Master.' The achievement, through the power of the Spirit, of balance of this kind will enable us to be experienced as 'grace-full' people.

The second word is *perspective*, and it follows naturally on the concept of balance. The more truly balanced we are, the more correct our perspective will be. It is when we are 'unbalanced' (the word is significant) that we lose our perspective and see things all out of proportion. The word 'perspective' is, by derivation, obviously related to the concept of 'looking through' and the Christian's 'looking through' events will be determined by the stance he takes up, for stance determines perspective. Our stance within the Christian faith will ensure that we see everything in relationship to the resources available from God through His Spirit. And clear in our sights from this perspective will be the need for balance and wholeness. The attainment of balance and perspective will be the prayer and the aim of souls growing in grace. The process will be greatly forwarded through creative silence.

The third word is '*non-conformity*' (non-conformity with a lower-case 'n'!). This may surprise but the point is important. Nothing I have said about balance turns it into conformity. Nothing I have said about lack of balance implies that we must never step out of line. The reverse is, indeed, the case. We may have to look fools for Christ's sake. We may have to emphasise apartness to make clear the difference from 'the world' that is required. We may have to walk separately to show where we are. We may even have to stand quite alone for Christ's sake. Jesus, the man of true balance, was different to the point of being unique, but it was precisely the perspective He had that compelled Him to be *nonconformist*. He was crucified because He just would not and could not conform to expectations.

It was His perspective and sense of balance that made Him nonconformist over Sabbath observance. Just because He had the right perspective on life and the ways of God, He could see that 'the Sabbath was made for man, not man for the Sabbath'. It was because He had an understanding of health and wholeness, based on the perspective of One who was 'Very God' but incarnate of the Virgin Mary, He could offer and accomplish healing miracles.

The ability to go against the tide which is 'nonconformity', is dependent on (the fourth concept) '*inner strength and peace*'. Standing alone, being 'apart' from the world is not an easy way to have to go. Yet it is the demand focussed in a sharp word to Peter, recorded at the end of John's Gospel. Peter was concerned as to what would happen to John. Jesus' response was as clear as it was pointed: 'What is that to thee? Follow thou me!' (John 21:22). It is the demand made of all of us. We must not measure the direction of our discipleship by looks over our shoulder to see where others are going or what others are doing. Jesus asks, simply, for obedience. 'Follow thou me!' That may well be a call to nonconformity. If it is, the strain on our interior strength will be real.

That strength is at hand. The Holy Spirit *is* the 'Comforter' and that by derivation means the

'Strengthener'. The gift of grace is there to be used. So the grace-full man and the grace-full woman will be enabled to take the path not taken by the masses, and see it as the fruit of true perspective and the sign of true balance.

*   *   *

In the silence comes the contact of the soul with Spirit. The seed is planted. Out of contact with the Spirit, new life in Christ grows. The seed is tended and watered. Out of new life there comes the harvest.

It is the harvest of the Spirit.

PART 2

THE HARVEST OF
THE SPIRIT

9

The Source of the Miracle of Grace

THE HARVEST of the Spirit is the magnificent phrase used in the *New English Bible* to describe what the *Authorised Version* calls 'the fruit of the Spirit' (Galatians 5:22). I want now to feel the impact of these magnificent words and the profound attitudes they represent, for, according to the letter to the Galatians from Paul, the harvest of the Spirit is 'love, joy, peace, patience, kindness, goodness, fidelity, gentleness and self-control'. And all these qualities are the produce of the life, nourished by creative silence and developed in the power of the Spirit. These are the products of grace. This is where we reap what the Spirit has sown.

The letter to the Galatians was possibly Paul's first letter to one of the communities for which he felt a responsibility. It contains, even in its short compass, the very essence of his teaching. It is passionate, personal and pointed, yet it is pastoral through and through. The pastor who loves his people will pull no punches over the fundamentals of faith. Yet always he will speak the truth in love. Paul did this to the Galatians.

The letter has several Pauline themes. It has, for example, a spirited defence of his apostleship. Paul, with the searing honesty that always compelled him to face the truth about himself, had no qualms about admitting his past. 'You have heard of my former career when the religion of the Jews was my religion', he says in Chapter I, verses 13 and 14 (WB). 'You are well aware that there were no bounds to my persecution of God's church and that I tried to blast it out of existence. In my fanatical enthusiasm for my ancestral traditions, I outstripped most of my contemporaries and my compatriots in the Jewish way of life and belief'. But he had no doubt about the validity of his apostleship or the source of his message. 'I owe my knowledge to no man's institution and to no man's teaching. No! It came to me by direct revelation from Jesus Christ' (1:12). Then he goes to the very centre of his position, the belief that was a direct product of his experience. There is only one way to 'get right with God'. That way is 'by faith' alone.

Paul's letter to the Galatians was intended to establish clearly and for ever, the essential message of the Gospel. 'No man can get into a right relationship with God by means of doing the things that any law prescribes. The only way to get into a right relationship with God is through faith in Christ Jesus' (2:16). We are not saved by works, but by grace. It is by faith alone we are 'justified'. 'In Christ's school we are made right with God through faith' (3:24). So the great doctrine of justification by faith has built itself into our view of the way we attain life. 'Salvation by works' is a counsel of despair. 'Salvation by faith' is a fanfare of hope. The harvest of the Spirit is not the merit through which we gain salvation. It is the product of the salvation we have — in Christ. It is the gift of grace.

The language I have been using may again sound to some old-fashioned, over-theological, out-of-date. 'Are you simply going to write off the *facts* of your faith?' Paul asks (3:4). It is the experience, not the form of language in which it is described that matters. If our own experience reflects the frustration and despair of trying to win divine blessing by our own efforts, we shall share with Paul the joy of the discovery that 'getting right with God' is about acceptance and gracious receiving. The historic word may be 'justification' but the experience it represents is authenticated acceptance by the gift of grace. The 'agent' is the Holy Spirit. 'It is by the help of the Spirit that we eagerly await the hoped-for right relationship with God which comes from faith.' (5:5). Such is the miracle of new creation. It is 'conversion' — the turning-point. The language may vary, the appropriateness of concepts may change, but the miracle of grace has been repeated a million times down the ages and it is being repeated again today. In Christ, there simply is a new creation, a new creature.

'If the Spirit is the ruling principle of our lives' (5:25) in our growth in grace, 'we must march in step with the Spirit'. Our growth in grace and in the likeness of Christ will come slowly but surely until we reap the harvest of the Spirit and begin to produce the fruit that bears testimony to the miracle within. 'I am not going to treat the grace of God as if it did not exist' (2:21).

*   *   *

What a striking statement that is! It comes in William Barclay's translation and it was made very emphatically. Its effect then must have been profound and dramatic. Its effect now is equally touching. We cannot hope to produce the harvest of the Spirit unless the grace of God *is* real *and* felt to be real. When that has happened, and that grace is a felt reality, the way to the production of the fruit of the Spirit is open.

God grant that what we are is not a complete denial of that grace! God grant that what we fail to be is contained within the enabling grace! God grant that we shall show, by the fruit of the Spirit in our lives, 'whose we are, and whom we serve'; that we are grace-full people.

It may be worth a short digression to say one word about the reality of grace, for we take our stand, set our course, initiate our stance — as I have said — by faith. In the realm with which we are dealing, logical and rational proof can never apply. We are discussing matters known to us by 'revelation', by intuition and instinct. Peter (as we have already noted) could not (Jesus said) have made his historic confession of Christ's Messiahship and Sonship without revelation from 'my Father which is in heaven'.

'Flesh and blood could not have revealed it unto thee' (Matthew 16:17). The knowledge we have is 'beyond knowledge' (Ephesians 3:19).

Christians are therefore in some difficulty over the stance they take because the reasons for that stance cannot be explained. Their convictions are, to the world, 'foolishness' and they are adjudged 'fools for Christ's sake'. Belief in and experience of the reality of grace is of the 'beyond knowledge' kind, and we must face all the implications of that in our testimony to it.

The grace of God exists and we know it. To live, act, think or feel as if that grace was not reality, is to deny the very source of spiritual life and growth. Justification (or spiritual 'turning-point') and 'sanctification' (spiritual growth) are impossible without the reality of that which we cannot prove, but by which we live and on which we base all. God was incarnate in Jesus Christ who died and rose again, who promised and sent the Holy Spirit as living, active energy. Not a word of this statement is 'provable' in human terms, but it is the source and ground of our life in the Spirit.

So then (our digression completed) we have repeated the fundamentals of our faith and we dare not treat them as if they were not true. Love divine exists. Grace abounds. New life is offered. We take our stand on these realities or we give up, for all time, the Gospel. The accusations of irrelevance and unreality that will be thrown at us are of no importance. Christians do not treat the grace of God as if it did not exist.

It is the reality of this grace that I am emphasising as we seek the emergence in our lives of 'the harvest of the Spirit'. For the production of love and joy and peace and all the other qualities we shall examine is not a simple task of will. It is possible only as grace abounds within. We cannot resolve to have 'the harvest of the Spirit'. We can, through grace, create the possibility of producing such fruit. It is not resolution but consecration that leads to such fruit. It is not effort but the acceptance of gift that makes it possible. It is not the flow of our adrenalin on demand that leads to good works. It is the flow of divine love in our being that is crucial.

Deep in our hearts — as there was in the Paul who first talked about the harvest of the Spirit — there is the awful conflict that arises from the presence of the 'fault' in our nature. Our reforming forefathers would have called it 'original sin', a phrase that is largely unacceptable to most people today. I do not defend the phrase itself, but I do believe it represents a concept that is profoundly true and valid — the built-in human inability to conquer evil and create good that only divine help can overcome. There are — as Paul was to find through the miracle of the Damascus road — factors relating to us that need not human resolution and effort, but divine grace. Saul of Tarsus, the man with a religious reputation and moral attainment, was a man without hope. Only when he became Paul the Christian could he feel the joy and freedom God promises. It needed a miracle of grace to 'save' him and make him all we know him to be.

It needs the miracle of grace to prepare the ground from which shall come the harvest of the Spirit. The harvest will be produced, not because we resolve but because we receive; not because we set ourselves new moral standards but because we ask for and find the grace that brings quality to life: not because we increase our 'good works' target, but because we allow the Spirit to flow through us in abundance.

> My will is not mine own
> Till Thou has made it Thine
> If it would reach a monarch's throne
> It must its crown resign

So George Matheson encapsulates the paradox that is, in human terms, foolishness, but which is, in divine terms, faith triumphant. The only way to growth and life is through death. The only way to victory is through surrender. The only way to resurrection is through the cross.

> And from the ground there blossoms red,
> Life that shall endless be.

10

Grace Abounding

THE HARVEST of the Spirit is the product of 'grace abounding' and the more grace abounds, so much greater shall the harvest be. Paul's letter to the Galatians is concentrated on the clash between 'faith' and 'works' and an understanding of the importance of the emphasis on 'faith alone' is so crucial for the life of faith and service, that I turn to it for a moment now.

Let us take note again of some of the most important sequences from Paul's letter that add light to our understanding of that which I am calling 'grace abounding'. They are all taken from William Barclay's translation of the letter.

'I am not going to treat the grace of God as if it did not exist' (2:21).

'Status symbols mean nothing to God' (2:6).

'God called me by His grace, and He chose to reveal His Son to me, and through me to others' (1:15–16).

'No man can get into a right relationship with God by means of doing the things which the law prescribes. The only way to get into a right relationship with God is through faith in Christ Jesus' (2:16).

'You began in the Spirit. Are you going to write off all the great facts of your Christian experience? Are you going to end up trying to win salvation by doing something to your body?' (3:4).

'The law was therefore the servant who brought us to the door of the school of Christ, so that in Christ's school we might be made right with God through faith' (3:24).

In other words, Paul's *experience*, allied to his *intuitional* understanding of the essence of the faith — a matter of revelation, not argument — and to his *intellectual* ability to 'theologise' the content of experience and revelation, left him in no doubt at all as to where the crux of the Gospel lay. It was in the opportunity, through grace alone, to attain to the stature and fullness of Christ. Any version of the faith which does not take its stand on that fundamental base will fail to express fully the essential Christian Gospel.

The 'school of Christ' is an important one for us all. There was a 'life-educational' value · in the law. Its function was to bring us to the door of the school of Christ, and show us the absolute necessity of something other than law in leading us to salvation and wholeness. In that preparatory school, Paul — or we should say Saul of Tarsus — had been thoroughly educated. The law as he realised with hindsight, was the schoolmaster (Galatians 3:24) that prepared him for and brought him to Christ. In that school, he had been an outstanding scholar and had built up an excellent pedigree. 'I might well base my claims on externals' he writes. 'If anyone thinks he can rely on physical marks and human achievement, I have an even stronger claim: I was circumcised on the eighth day after I was born. I am a pure-blooded Israelite. I am a Hebrew and the son of Hebrew parents. I belong to the tribe of Benjamin. In my attitude to the Jewish law, I was a Pharisee. So enthusiastic was my devotion to the law that I was a persecutor of the Church. As far as the goodness which the law prescribes and demands are concerned, I was beyond criticism. But whatever achievement in my life and career I would once have reckoned among the profits of life, I have written off as a dead loss for the sake of Christ. Yes, and more than that, I am prepared to write off everything as a dead loss for the sake of getting to know Christ Jesus, my Lord' (Philippians 3:4–8 WB).

I have deliberately tried to let Paul speak for himself on this crucial matter before taking the example of his 'justification by faith' (that is of finding again a right relationship with God) and the subsequent 'sanctification' in his life (that is growth in grace through the Spirit) into our own experience. What has been so crucial to a theological understanding of the implications of the Gospel in the life of the church is the record of this brilliant man of outstanding intellect and achievement, who had a profound understanding of the human dilemma, placing *everything* on the free gift of grace in Jesus Christ, through the Spirit. 'If the Spirit,' says Paul, 'is the ruling principle of our lives, we must march in step with the Spirit' (5:25 WB). The battle to secure balance between 'flesh' and 'spirit' is never over, but it is being won if the Spirit is 'the rule of your life'. To walk, as on a journey or a pilgrimage, in the Spirit guarantees a richer harvest than we can ever imagine in advance. There will surely be love, joy, peace, patience, kindness and goodness.

'The only way then to get into a right relationship with God is through faith in Christ Jesus.' This so clear and defined — even dogmatic — statement by Paul is, as I have said, the cornerstone of the theology of the Christian and, as I have emphasised all through the book, it is out of that grace-full relationship alone, the harvest can come. It cannot be produced by effort, discipline or duty. It grows out of the co-operation, through grace, of 'God-with-us' — Emmanuel (Matthew 1:23).

* * *

The glory in such a doctrine is the anxiety it takes away from us all for it divorces salvation from meritorious effort and achievement and grounds it in grace alone. The danger it carries — as it did in Galatia and Corinth — is of a confusion between liberty and licence that could be soul-destroying.

Let us look at both of these points, drawing comfort from the first and asking for caution in relation to the second.

In relation to the first, let me go back to the point I made earlier — that the doorway to the new liberty Paul found on, or soon after the Damascus road, was his own *experience*. 'The Gospel which I preach is no human affair. I owe my knowledge to no man's instruction and to no man's teaching. No! It came direct to me by direct revelation from Jesus Christ' (Galatians 1:11–12 WB). Paul experienced the utmost in personal agony in his efforts to please God by moral attainment, legal correctness and human achievement. The liberty came ('O wretched man that I am! Who shall deliver me from this death?') when Paul saw that the law could not cure his spiritual condition. The law showed him what sin was. The law showed a man his sin. The law defined sin. The law made man conscious of his sin. But the law could not *cure* sin. It was there that the dilemma thrown up in the preparatory school of the Law lay. Only in the school of Christ was peace possible. There alone was grace abounding.

Paul's conversion is not a psychological phenomenon to be explained away in terms of a guilt or other 'complex'. It was a life-changing experience that, examined by that highly able mind reflecting on the whole of his life's journey and the dramatic events that re-directed it, attributed it all, through the 'knowledge that is beyond knowledge', to the action of God in Christ. The man in bondage to the law became the man who, through grace was free. Relationship to God, obscured by the impossible pressure to attain to perfection by works, was illumined in the realisation that, to those with faith grace is free, unearned, undeserved. The strains of the striving, the stress of the struggling, the anxiety of attainment attempted against the inner 'forces of sin' belongs to the past. 'He called me by His grace.'

The second point — the danger of confusing liberty with licence — has always been present where there is immaturity in religious experience and understanding. It is always possible to argue that we can sin more 'so that grace may the more abound'. But this is a misunderstanding of the responsibilities of true liberty. Freedom involves not anarchy but discipline. Grace does not allow us to do as we like. It enables us to do 'as God likes', in a way we could not do it before.

So the doctrine of salvation 'by faith alone' is, I repeat, not a passport to licence. It is a demand that, knowing a new freedom, we be the more disciplined and responsible. Only through such discipline can we produce the harvest of the Spirit, for that harvest is the outward confirmation of the Spirit working in us. The Spirit does bring fruit out of the responsibility of the redeemed Christian, but could have no effect on the uncontrolled licence of 'go-as-you-please' behaviour.

It is important to realise that the Holy Spirit produces order and balance in a life, not disorder, disharmony or destruction. Where disorder is present and the Holy Spirit's presence is claimed, we must always be on our guard. The Spirit does produce excitement and ecstasy on occasion but whatever it produces must, in the end, show itself to be a contribution to a rounded Christian life. This does not mean, of course, that the mark of the spiritual life is a dull conformity. I have already emphasised the call to nonconformity in Christian witness. There is plenty of room for divine eccentricity and enthusiastic individualism in the service of the Kingdom. How otherwise can we ever become fools for Christ's sake? But beneath and around the kind of life in which there is evidence of the harvest of the Spirit, there is a balance, an order, a harmony and a wholeness that is very convincing. It is all that which witnesses to the divine presence and blesses this world.

So the great Gospel becomes a framework and a structure for 'life abundant'. The great words in its vocabulary take on meaning and the great events that make up God's 'plan of salvation' become real. Each one is an element in the process that brings about the right relationship with God which is His will and His purpose. The statements in creeds make sense. The mysteries of 'three-in-one and one-in-three' are not verbal puzzles but a summary of the facts which are real in our experience. There is one God and we have come to know Him as Father. There is one Saviour, Jesus Christ, the Son of God, whom we have met as the stranger of Galilee and the cosmic Christ. There is the divine Holy Spirit, the energy of God promised and given to be with us always. How else can Christians express their faith when their experience is of God coming to us in three ways, yet being the one, indivisible God? The paradox must be maintained where finite words endeavour to contain infinite truth. So is it too with the natures of our Lord. How can anyone be Son of God and Son of man as they claimed Jesus was? But again we face a mystery. He was! Peter's declaration has been followed by millions since. 'Thou art the Christ, the Son of the Living God.' Yet He was one of us. 'He suffered . . . and was tempted like as we are.' We have been shown mysteries but, by faith, we know they represent truth.

The harvest of the Spirit is the produce of the miracle of grace, freely offered by God, available through Jesus Christ our Lord, developed through the working of the eternal Holy Spirit. The relationship man broke is healed on the initiative of God. The fruits of the restored relationship are just such things as love and joy and peace and patience and kindness and goodness and commitment and self-control. They whisper His presence and they shout His praise.

11

Love, Joy, Peace

THE FIRST-FRUIT of the harvest of the Spirit is Love. It is the most fundamental of Christian qualities, for God is Love. It is the quality that suffers long and is kind, that envies not, that does not vaunt itself and is not puffed up with pride, that does not behave itself in an unseemly way, nor does it seek its own advantage. It is not easily irritated and it does not think evil of any. It bears, believes, hopes and endures all things. It never fails. Love 'lasts for ever'. It is the ground of 'the Golden Rule': 'Thou shalt love the Lord Thy God with heart and soul and mind and strength and thy neighbour as thy self.'

Love is of God, so not surprisingly the greatest of all the gifts of the Spirit is love. So it is always the first fruit in the harvest of the Spirit.

*   *   *

It would take a book on its own to give any kind of exposition of love. I hope that book will (as I said in the Preface) come in due course. Here I confine myself to underlining some of the essential characteristics of love, the first-fruit in the harvest of the Spirit.

'God is Love.' 'Love is of God.' These statements from the New Testament on the centrality of love are fundamental to any attempt to describe what God is like. They therefore indicate where love comes in the divine perspective. The great commandments are about love — love to God and love to our neighbour. Where we run into difficulties is finding out how to proclaim this concept in a word that is understood, for the word 'love' has to cover, in English, a multitude of biblical uses and a wide spectrum of meaning.

The confusion arising from that has made the use of the word 'love' a worry because it may be misunderstood. Love in the sense of the Greek word 'eros' and love in the sense of the Greek word 'agape' have become confused in the minds of people, who, influenced by ideas familiar to earlier eras, are still afraid of the word and the idea of 'love'. It has therefore been a sad fact of Christian history and congregational life in our times that any sign of 'loving-ness' between people is suspect and open to possible criticism. If two people, who are not married, are seen to be loving towards each other, whispers of suspicion begin to be heard. If two women or two men are noticeably 'fond of each other', hands of horror are raised. If priest and nun affect a loving relationship although it is technically consonant with their vows of celibacy, the Christian community wonders anxiously 'what is happening'. It is often not a question of 'seeing how these Christians love one another'. It is asking anxious questions if they do.

It may well be said that the sort of attitudes I describe are what used to be, but no longer characterise church life. I think there is validity in that claim. Expressed affection, loving embraces and greater understanding between men and women, women and women, and men with men, are much more acknowledged features of many areas of Christian community, though I suspect the degree to which this is so is very variable from community to community, in different cultural bands, from church to church, etc. What does appear to be the case is that love is more 'recognised' than it has been, and that can only be a gain.

What has helped this recognition come about has been the clarification of the 'physical' or sexual aspect of love. The misapprehension that love equals sex ('making love') has seriously damaged the recognition of Christian love in its own right. So long as any kind of touching or familiarity has had 'physical' overtones — as it has had for great sections of people in Christian churches — the limitations on the expression of love have been enormous. Through 'charismatic renewal' on one hand and new concepts of pastoral care on the other — representing very different theological approaches — greater acceptance of expressed love has been possible.

I do not make the separation of love and physical relationship total, for the proper end of deep and sincere love is a relationship of 'togetherness' on every level — spiritual, emotional and physical, the last within the context of total and committed love, but I do feel the recognition of love as the element that makes true Christian relationship, without seeing it as necessarily involving 'the sexual element' in it, has increased. Christianity is based on loving relationship between God, ourselves and our neighbour. This is 'the eternal triangle' that is grounded wholly on the love which is of God (as I have noted earlier). Let that love be recognised, acknowledged and expressed in worship, fellowship and service. Ours is the Gospel of Love.

Love is then that corpus of outgoing attitudes that all arise from the attitude of God to us. It embraces compassion, empathy, sympathy, understanding, forgiveness, acceptance, grace-fullness, concern, and caring because God first gave us every one of these gifts and continues to do so. It is a reaching out, arms outstretched in welcome, for in this very way, God 'first' loved us.

The next element that is love in these terms is its 'enabling', not compelling, quality. Love does not dominate. It cultivates.

Again this is an attitude based directly on the way God deals with us. For specific examples we turn to the incident involving the rich young ruler (Matthew 19:16–22) and the story of the Prodigal Son (Luke 15: 11–32).

In both cases we have a demonstration of cultivation

rather than domination. The Prodigal Son is allowed to go to 'a far country', to make his mistakes and to stay there until he 'comes to himself' and makes for home. It is the distance itself that contributes to the miracle of grace. The rich young ruler is allowed by Jesus to go away and no pressure of any kind is put on him. This is the way God's love deals with people. It respects their right of personality. It allows them the decision-making process. It seeks for response, not blind obedience.

This is the kind of 'enabling' love the Christian is asked to develop. But it is not easy to carry out! So often unconscious factors operate in our relationships with people. So often there are unconscious pressures coming from within ourselves to *use* people rather than to enable them. So we make the mistake of using people as *means* rather than treating them as having an inherent importance. God respects personality. We too must avoid the abuse of people to further our own ends. It will always be of the nature of love to cultivate.

I cannot leave love without relating it specifically to compassion. Compassion is outgoing sensitivity and empathy that actually turns into *action*. 'And Jesus, moved with compassion, put forth His hand...' 'When Jesus saw the multitudes, He was moved with compassion: ...' (Mark 1:41, 6:34).

Compassion is, by derivation, a 'suffering with' somebody. It is recognisable as a distinctive feeling warming up in the heart when some situation presents itself to us, or some individual is in deep need. It is felt where there is a factor present that grazes the soul or touches the deep places of our being. The feelings are subjective and within, but their characteristic, where compassion is expressed, is their objectivity. There is a real reason for the compassion to which we are moved.

This is not the love that identifies in a way that brings 'emotional involvement'. It is not the love that moves on to a relationship of longer or even shorter duration. It is a love which carries no implications beyond the compassion it feels. It does not necessarily imply any 'on-going' responsibility. It is the out-flow of the moment, in response to need or pain or suffering or bereavement or hurt. Sincerely offered, it brings the blessing of the moment. Having been given from the soul, in that moment, and expressed in whatever action is appropriate, we move on to that next thing we have to do, that moment that may move us to compassion again.

Our moments of compassion may come seldom or often, but when they do, they are expressing something which is of the healing attribute of God Himself. It is a sign of the presence of the healing Spirit within. It is Love in action.

So love is a serving that seeks no return, no thanks, no honour. Love is the tireless touch that tells another 'I am here'. Love is the capacity to suffer with another, to give, to retire unnoticed, ready only to answer the call of need again.

Love is indeed the first-fruit of the harvest of the Spirit.

*   *   *

'Blessed is the man that walketh not in the counsel of the ungodly, nor standeth in the way of sinners nor sitteth in the seat of the scornful: but his delight is in the law of the Lord: and in His law doth he meditate day and night. He shall be like a tree planted by the water that bringeth forth fruit in his season' (Psalm 1:1–3a).

Joy — his delight — is the second fruit in the harvest of the Spirit and joy comes through a healthy relationship between God and man.

The dictionary definitions of joy fall short of the full measure given to 'joy' in the Bible. Joy is, the dictionary says, 'the emotion produced by gratified desire, success, happy fortune'. It is mirth, gaiety — and so on. Only when it goes on to speak of joy as happiness, gladness, delight and exultation, does it begin to reach something of the Bible's profound understanding of joy.

'Gratified desire' has very 'physical' connotations. If the phrase has any relevance at all to Biblical joy, it must include the 'spiritualising' of that concept. Joy, in Christian terms, is related to the 'gratified desire' of the soul and spirit for relationship with God. It *is* related to a 'healthy' relationship with God — a relationship of wholeness. 'Gratified desire' at any level short of the desires of the soul will not produce joy — as the true seeker of life discovers. 'Man does not live by bread alone.' Many who marry to gratify desire discover, not so far along the way (as many younger people are now affirming) that, passion spent, the search for real joy and meaning begins.

Joy, the fruit of the Spirit, is therefore no superficial emotion, no noisy expression of amusement, no passing engagement in pleasure-providing play. It is a quality, deep in our inner being, of smiling radiance, a product of the presence of the peace that passes understanding, a reflection of reconciliation felt through a relationship received by the redemptive activity of grace. It is a true fruit of the Spirit.

Joy, as an inner quality rather than an outward emotional or physical expression, is an attribute of God Himself, so human joy is a reflection of Divine joy just as love is a reflection of the Divine love. God rejoices in His works (Psalm 104:31). God rejoices over His people reconciled and restored to relationship (for example, Deuteronomy 30:9). 'God shall rejoice over you as a young man rejoices over his bride' (Isaiah 62:5). 'The Lord your God will rejoice over you and be glad: He will show you His love once more' (Zephaniah 3:17).

In the New Testament, the supreme Divine joy is again related to reconciliation, the lost found, the dead restored to true life. 'There is joy among the angels of God over one sinner who repents.' 'There will be greater joy in heaven over one sinner who repents than over ninety and nine who do not need to repent' (Luke 15:10 and 7). So the Divine joy is expounded throughout the New Testament: 'I have spoken this to you (that is about Divine Love) so that joy may be in you and your joy complete' (John 15:11). 'I speak these words so that they (the disciples) may have my joy within them in full measure' (John 17:13). And supremely — for the Incarnation is an event of Divine joy — 'I bring you good tidings of great joy for unto you is born this day in the city of David, a Saviour who is Christ, the Lord.' (Luke 2:10).

Paul brings joy then to the centre of the Gospel he preaches. The Christian is to 'rejoice always' (I Thessalonians 5:16) and that 'always' includes joy in adversity (Romans 5:3–11, Colossians 1:24). Remember, too, Peter who wrote on this theme in his first letter (1:6–12). Indeed, triumphant victory through adversity is evidence of the ultimate all-embracing joy that is to come. So (as Revelation tells us pictorially and symbolically) there is the 'singing' of 'a new song' when the powers of darkness are conquered.

The joy that is of the harvest of the Spirit is then a profound quality of being, a product of grace and faith. It is not an ethereal quality associated only with the soul and certainly not just a pleasurable gratification associated with the body. It is a joy *related to our wholeness* which cannot be felt unless our deepest spiritual needs are met, but which is rightly felt also in the delight of the senses when dedicated to the glory of God.

*   *   *

'But I will call upon God: the Lord will save me ... He has heard my cry ... and gave me back my peace.' So writes the Psalmist (Psalm 55: 16–18, NEB) in gratitude for the recovery of something he had lost. The blessing lay in the restoration of true and lasting inner peace.

Inner peace is a product of the harvest of the Spirit. Of all the fruits of the Spirit, I am just touching on (for, as I have said, their full development requires a very large book!) peace is perhaps the most profound. 'Our hearts are rest-less till they rest in Thee.' The heart cries out for relationship restored. The soul yearns for the union fractured by our waywardness. The whole of our being 'groans' (the Psalmist uses the word as well as Paul) to be at one and so to be at peace with God . . . and, of course, by implication with our 'neighbours'. So the language of theology, the vocabulary of the mission-hall, the symbols of worship and the images of true contemplation join to proclaim the same desire and the same longing. While it may be described in the 'spiritual song' as 'There's none but Christ can satisfy' or it may be seen as the full union the mystic understands, the fundamental experience is the same. Jesus Christ *is* the Way, the Truth and the Life. He *is* the author of the 'peace which the world cannot give'. Relationship is restored 'by grace alone' and so our peace is 'given back' to us through reconciliation. The Spirit is at work. The harvest *is* peace.

Peace, the Psalmist says, is the recovery of something lost. 'He gave me *back* my peace.' In the traditional devotional language of Christianity, the ideal divine-human relationship has been destroyed by sin. Mankind lost his right to relationship (as the 'myths' — in the technical sense — of Genesis tell us) by his desire to 'be as God'. That was the cardinal sin in that story. In more contemporary concepts, the cumulative 'shadow' of the individual and collective unconscious (to use Jung's terms) creates negative psychic influences that set up barriers, on the human side . . . between man and God. So the 'fault' (using this word in the geological sense, metaphorically) which is the result of 'the Fall' in traditional theological language, or the 'block' if we use contemporary psychological jargon, continues until a new energy, or in Christian language, grace breaks down the barriers to communion, relationship and union, the gifts always 'on offer' to mankind. It is this basic 'justification by faith', this removal of the 'blocks' by divine initiative, this reconciliation possible where faith responds to offered grace in Christ, through the Spirit, that 'converts', 'redeems', 'saves', 'reconciles', brings about 'new birth', opens the door to 'union', makes possible individuation, allows integration . . . in whatever terms we like to put it. It is from the platform of that 'justification by faith' that 'sanctification', 'regeneration', 'life abundant', evolves . . . through the presence and power of the Holy Spirit. The product of the central miracle of grace is a deep, inner peace, a peace 'that passes understanding'.

The presence of such peace in a life has profound practical effects. One is an ability to cope with criticism in such a way that we are able to continue creatively, despite opposition, hostility and even ridicule. We are also enabled to cope with time pressure without breakdown. The strength of that inner peace can be enough to bring perspective where there might well be panic; can enable one to accept that 'sufficient unto the day' is all we have to face: can provide an unruffled calm in the face of decisions that must be made, can enable the sleep that is essential when others have only 'sleepless nights'.

Another consequence of inner peace is a sense of purpose in relation to God's providence. It is hard in the kind of world in which we live to feel the meaningfulness of life at all, to be convinced that good will, in any sense, triumph over evil, that 'the kingdoms of this world' can become the kingdom of our Lord and Saviour, Jesus Christ. Peace brings again perspective, a perspective that sees more clearly the divine estimate of time, that enables us to put events *sub specie aeternitatis* — in the context of eternity — and timelessness. There cannot be confidence and peace within if we survey history and 'the news' from 'floor' level. The unfolding panorama of violence, war, want, prejudice, terrorism, murder, rape gives no ground for hope. Only by taking a standpoint outside daily happenings can we begin to see the purpose of God within the workings of human history, the possibilities for good amidst so much evil, and the certainty of the ultimate triumph of grace in the world. This is not for one moment to diminish the awfulness of life as we know it or to deny the terrible reality of the forces of evil in the world and in the universe, but it is to see the whole from another 'angle of vision' and from that stance find some encouragement. 'We shall not be moved' they sing. These words, re-interpreted, are true for all who acquire true peace. There is a sustaining strength that enables serenity and tranquillity to be where there ought to be, in human terms, fear and trembling. 'Thou wilt keep him in perfect peace, whose mind is stayed on Thee.'

Nothing I have said means that we should not reduce the pressures that are too great to enclose within the time and strength we have available. On the practical ground that we shall never do things well if we try to do too much, we must review our undertakings in God's service. Nor do I suggest that we should never 'hear' our critics. What we need not do is react, or over-react, to criticism. We take what is valid and reject what is not. As a result, we may well improve something we are doing. But we no longer feel we *have* to accept criticism. Perhaps the model for us all, of perfect peace, under pressure, is the occasion when Jesus stood before His accusers. Their impertinent and even blasphemous questions were hurled at Him. But 'He answered them nothing'. This is what the psychologists call ego-strength. This is what the Christian feels as God's peace within. To be despised and rejected is never easy for any of us. It makes us into men and women of sorrow and it acquaints us with grief. It is not easy to be rejected by group or loved one. But true inner peace can enable us to cope with even total rejection.

So the product of the harvest of the Spirit that peace is, is vital to our well-being. With this peace which the world cannot give, within us, our hearts need not be troubled, neither need they ever be afraid.

12

Patience, Meekness, Goodness

AS WITH OTHER fruits of the Spirit, the qualities a Christian is expected to produce are reflections of attributes first demonstrated, albeit on a scale far above our possible attainment, by God Himself. Love must be evident in a Christian's life because God is Love and first loved us. Joy is to be a reflection of the divine joy. Peace is a direct consequence of the gift of the peace of God which the world can neither give (as I said above) nor take away. Similarly *patience* is demanded of us — or 'long suffering' as the *Authorised Version* describes it — because the model for our patience is the patience of God.

God is a 'long-suffering' God — but not in the slightly negative sense that particular word seems to imply. This is, in itself, a reason for my preference for the word 'patience'. He *is* the God of patience, and that patience is a redemptive and creative quality, concerned only with the ultimate bringing back of the perverse soul to the Divine embrace. We can, then, best feel the need to learn true patience by understanding the essential meaning of that Divine yearning for the ultimate good of His people.

The Divine patience is grounded (the word patience itself is related etymologically to 'suffering') in grace and not in law or right. The whole weight of the Gospel, as I have been declaring it throughout this book, is founded and built on a premise, fundamental to all Paul proclaims as a result of his own experience. It is that, given the broken relationship which man, in his freedom has effected, the restoration of that relationship cannot be demanded by man as a right and cannot be earned by man as a reward. It can only be offered by God as an act of grace. That offer is made, but our 'perverse and foolish' rejection of it, due to both our personal sin and our collective sinfulness ('I am a man of unclean lips and I dwell in the midst of a people of unclean lips' — Isaiah 6:5) commits God to wait and wait and wait. We are, returning to the Prodigal Son, allowed to go to the far country while the Father waits patiently and lovingly. The rich young ruler (we note again) is allowed to go away, perhaps later to ruminate on response, refusal, regret and even perhaps remorse, aware that it is not the Divine way to overwhelm personality against our will, that it is of the essence of the Divine will to long, to yearn, to *wait* in order ultimately to receive. 'There is joy in heaven over one sinner who repents' I repeat. The Prodigal Son was 'dead and is alive again. He was lost and is found.'

It is this attitude of God that is, in the creative sense of the word, 'long-suffering' for it does imply real suffering in the heart of God. 'Love suffers long.' That is the mark of the Divine patience. On it our human patience, the product of the harvest of the Spirit, must be grounded, impossible though it may be for us to emulate it. We are called, in our attitude to difficult, hostile or misunderstanding relationships, to be ready and willing to wait — wait patiently for a change of heart, a flicker of understanding, a hint of appreciation, a 'movement towards' of a reaching out and reconciling kind.

Such an attitude is a positive, creative, redemptive longing. It is the radiation of a readiness for reconciliation, the announcement of those open doors and outstretched arms. It does not exclude 'confrontation' within a relationship. It is where difference develops in situations of non-communication that danger lies. True relationship involves two living and active separate personalities able to disagree *and* maintain relationship. Reconciliation is the first step on the road to relationship recreated.

It is God's will that (as Paul says in I Timothy, 2:4) 'all men be saved and come to a knowledge of the truth'. In the end, all will return to the God who made them — if, like the Prodigal Son, they can come to themselves.

So God waits in patience for His recalcitrant people, not in anger or irritation, but with the Divine longing that lies eternally at His heart. We are asked to reproduce something of that patience in our lives. To do that means drawing on the resources of the Spirit.

Patience is not a natural human virtue. It can however come to be in us, a gift from God, through grace.

*   *   *

The word 'meekness' is one that is difficult for us, because of the 'feel' it has in English. It has been made equal to 'mild, submissive, humble, tame' (Cassells' Dictionary), but this is not at all the Bible's understanding of the word, so another translation must be found for it.

'Meekness' in the Bible, is not of the 'gentle Jesus, meek and mild' self-effacing mildness or weak submissiveness it sounds to be. It has to do with the concepts of lowliness, distress, poverty (in material terms) and abasement in the sense of 'low-estate'. So God is the champion of those afflicted by the world. 'The poor man cried, and the Lord heard him, and saved him out of all his troubles' (Psalm 34:6).

The 'meek shall inherit the earth' indeed, for God has special blessings for them. They may have a situation in life that is lowly, but, given that they have — and often did have — a trustful, humble attitude of mind, 'all will be well, all will be truly well'. So to be 'meek' is to submit oneself willingly to God's will at all times. It is a quality typical of the truly devoted spirit. 'Meekness' is the attitude of those devout souls who 'waited for the consolation of Israel' (Luke 2:25).

Jesus had no hesitation in identifying Himself with meekness in this biblical sense. It was a characteristic of His kingly and His messianic role. When He entered Jerusalem, He came 'meek and sitting on an ass'

(Matthew 21:5) just as the prophet Zechariah had promised (9:9).

Paul, in that great Philippians passage on the Humility of Christ (Philippians 2) underlines the true meekness of Christ, His true poverty, His trust in God, His humility. The Christ, who is cosmic in that He existed 'in the beginning', who was incarnate and lived a truly human life, who rose again having become 'obedient unto death, even death on a cross', is, in His acceptance of the whole spectrum of suffering, truly 'meek'.

What word can we then substitute for 'meekness'? The *New English Bible*, the *Jerusalem Bible* and the *Revised Version* offer 'gentleness', while *J. B. Phillips* suggests 'tolerance'. For me, it is once again *William Barclay* who boldly offers not a word, but a phrase, and gives us 'the strength of gentleness'. I have no doubt that it is in the paradoxical relationship of strength to gentleness that the real meaning of this product of the harvest of the Spirit lies.

This is confirmed by the use of the Greek word for 'meek' which means 'under control'. That is where J. B. Phillips sees 'tolerance' as a possible translation. But behind it there is always the general biblical emphasis of humble obedience to the divine will.

The strength of gentleness! What a glorious concept! How true it is of the Christ who walked this earth! How true it is of God Himself! 'He shall feed His flock like a shepherd, He shall gather the lambs with His arms, and carry them in His bosom, and shall gently lead those that are with young' (Isaiah 40:11). To that we must surely add the wonderful words from Ezekiel, especially as they are rendered in the *New English Bible* (34:15–16): 'I will search for the lost, recover the straggler, bandage the hurt, strengthen the sick, leave the healthy and strong to play and give them their proper food.' Surely there in the Old Testament 'the strength of gentleness' is present, and from there it is carried through to the New Testament where the Son of God is the 'Good Shepherd' who has the strength to give His life for the sheep. And He did.

This is then a gift of the Spirit for which we must all yearn. The true Christian is the gentle-man, the gentle-woman. There is a tenderness about their attitudes that conveys itself powerfully, both in relationship and in healing. There is, as Rupert Brooke tells us, 'gentleness in hearts at peace'.

There is perhaps something of importance emerging in that last quotation that we should note here. The more we dig deeper into the full meaning of the gifts of the Spirit, the more it is clear that each impinges on the other. It is out of inner peace that the capacity to express the strength of gentleness comes. It is out of love that goodness comes — and joy, and patience. The developed Christian life is a rounded life, a balanced life, an ordered life, for the Holy Spirit brings order and balance while the symbol of wholeness is a circle — a rounded line. This is not a recipe for conformity, or caution — far from it. Some of the most nonconformist Christians, full of the Spirit, have been the most balanced in their own way. What I seek to stress is the strong, solid base the Spirit creates, given the chance, and the calm, serene peace that base allows. From there all is possible!

Perhaps the last word on the strength of gentleness can come not from the Bible, but from Shakespeare (in *As You Like It*):

'Let gentleness my strong enforcement be'

*   *   *

What is goodness? To ask that question is to raise one of the historic questions that have occupied philosophers from time immemorial, yet surprisingly when I looked up my *Dictionary of the Bible* (Hastings, revised by Grant and Rowley), I found no entry 'goodness' in it at all. All the other products of the harvest of the Spirit that we have discussed are there — love, joy, peace, long-suffering (patience) and kindness — but not goodness. I wonder why, for it is one of the great indefinable concepts. It is notable, too, that while there are variations in terminology in the various versions of the Bible for other words, there is no real variation in relation to 'goodness'.

Goodness feels as if it had direct links with 'God-ness'. It is about all that is 'divine'. It therefore must be built around, on and within love for God *is* Love. Goodness is essentially an expression of God-ness and so is Love. For that reason, goodness is more in the area of an attribute than an attainment, more related to values than to morals.

This brings me to one of the most important comments we can make about goodness, for it takes us deep down to the lower levels, the foundations, perhaps even the cornerstone of our life system. As is the case with so much that is desirable in spiritual areas, goodness becomes less attainable the more we *try* to attain it, for goodness is, as I have said, a product, not an achievement. It shows itself naturally if the Spirit is at work within. It is part of the evidence of the harvest of the Spirit, the result of the Spirit's energies. It is most visible to others when we cannot see it in ourselves. It impinges most on the world when we are unaware that we are proclaiming it.

This profound truth lies at the very heart of the witness of the Reformers. It was the *theological* lynch-pin of the Reformation. So much did the pioneers of reformation emphasise it, that it became, in relation to the prime concept of *justification by faith alone*, one of the rocks on which reformation was built. Goodness is not the merit we create and offer to God as a claim for recognition. It is that which is created in us, increasingly in the process of sanctification, through the miracle of grace. So if goodness be seen to be part of our offering to the world, the credit goes, not to us, but the Spirit who works in us. That makes the possession of goodness a matter of profound humility. Goodness comes from the God-ness we meet in the incarnate Jesus and it is developed under the power of the Holy Spirit. Goodness is evidence of 'the Christ within'.

Goodness is therefore something to be longed for and looked for, but it is only possible to attain to it, through the miracle of grace and after it. How dramatically — and traumatically — Paul learned this on the Damascus Road! Goodness, is, I repeat, always the fruit of God's grace working within us. It reflects the goodness of the only wholly Good One, God ('Why callest thou me good? There is none good but one, that is God' said Jesus (Matthew 19:17) to the rich young ruler). Such goodness is part of the harvest of the Spirit.

In placing goodness so deeply within the operation of the Spirit and seeing it as an attribute rather than an achievement, I have, it may seem, set aside the concept of goodness as the equivalent of moral success. This, some may feel, is akin to many current emphases that put great stress on love and little on law, that make much of care and little of discipline, talk much of acceptance but little of demand. I understand this and have real sympathy with the anxiety that is to be expressed over such humanistic and quasi-spiritual concepts of love. But morals — that is the *mores* of a community, the acceptable behaviour of the community at any one period, in any particular culture are always *less* than goodness. They can even be misleading in relation to true goodness — as the attitudes and behaviour of the scribes and Pharisees in the lifetime of Jesus showed. It was precisely for this reason that Jesus made such searing attacks on the self-proclaimed religious and moral individuals and groups of his time. Those who came to point the finger at 'the woman taken in adultery' or 'the woman of bad reputation' who invaded the dinner party at the house of Simon the Pharisee were 'moral' but not good. The two women were 'good' but not moral. The defenders of morality in fact knew little about true religion — which is concerned with·

goodness. This is one of the most damning indictments ever made on those who offer a rigid morality as the goodness of God and all self-proclaimed religious people should take warning from it.

The same, as I have already said, was so true of St. Paul. The man with the moral and religious pedigree that was beyond criticism, had to learn that goodness, the product he proclaimed as part of the harvest of the Spirit, was something different and something greater, something much nearer the essence of divinity, God-ness.

Society may well need a higher morality than it has now. The mores of the community would gain from more self-discipline and more adherence to time-honoured standards. But in the end it will be the offering of sheer goodness that will bring quality into society and happiness to its members.

Jesus brought many blessings into life when 'the Word was made flesh and dwelt among us'. Perhaps the revelation in Himself of sheer goodness was one of the greatest. 'Good Master', said the rich young ruler, addressing Him. Jesus felt it necessary to divert this sincere statement in order to point him to the source and expression of true goodness, but nevertheless the rich young ruler, in his spontaneous adoration and respect, was expressing what people felt when they met the man, Jesus. 'Truly this was the Son of God', said the centurion at the Cross. The divine goodness was incarnate in Him and self-evident.

13

Faith, Kindness, Temperance

I HAVE NOT felt it necessary to take the products of the harvest of the Spirit strictly in their scriptural sequence. 'Meekness', for example, has already had our attention. We move now to the three remaining qualities not yet discussed . . . 'faith', 'gentleness' (for which I prefer the NEB and WB rendering 'kindness') and 'temperance'.

It will help to turn to various translations and versions of the New Testament to locate just what St. Paul was describing in these individual products in the harvest of the Spirit. We begin with 'faith'.

'Faith' is a word which like the English word 'love', has many meanings — and many shades of meaning. It is undeniably one of the most important and profound words in the Bible for it stands at the centre — as we have seen — of Reformed theology, with its fundamental emphasis on 'salvation by faith alone'. Is it that central concept of 'faith' that is in Paul's mind here?

Dr. William Barclay gives us four shades of meaning in the New Testament use of the word faith ('pistis' in Greek). It can mean, and indeed its main meaning is the characteristically Pauline concept of 'total commitment to Jesus Christ — accepting Christ at His word, both in His demands and in His promises' (see, for example, Galatians 2:16, 3:24, 3:26 — justification by faith). It may mean, secondly, 'unshakable hope', 'the substance of things hoped for' as in Hebrews 11:1. It may mean, thirdly, 'acceptance of certain propositions' in an intellectual way as in Hebrews 11:6. Fourthly it may be used, as it is in the phrase 'the Christian faith' (Galatians 1:23, 3:7, Jude verse 20). But in Galatians 5:22–24 the theme verses of our study, it is used to mean 'fidelity' or 'keeping faith'.

This is confirmed by the variations in translation in some of the other versions of the Bible, or New Testament. The *New English Bible* and *J. B. Phillips* have 'fidelity' as Dr. Barclay has. The *Revised Standard Version* uses the word 'faithfulness' and the *Jerusalem Bible* 'trustfulness'.

Here again I underline the point that I have made so often in this section of this book. The quality that *we* must have as evidence of the presence of the Spirit in our lives is a reflection of something that is an attitude of God. The call to 'love' arises because 'God is Love' and 'He first loved us'. The Divine joy precedes our human joy. The peace we long to demonstrate will be, in some way, a reflection of the Divine peace. The demand for patience pre-supposes the patience of a 'long-suffering' God. The call to be kind is based on the Divine kindness. The life of goodness is a reflection, at a very human level, of the Divine goodness.

When we come to 'faith' in the sense of 'fidelity', we come once more to a fundamental attribute of God. 'O Thou who changest not . . .' 'The same yesterday, today and for ever'. David, in his distress, 'encouraged himself in the Lord, his God' and this, I feel, was related to David's absolute certainty that God, by His very nature, could never let His servants down and would not do it now.

There is an innate constancy and consistency about God that does not allow of whim or unreliability. The God of Abraham, Isaac and Jacob is a God of loyalty. The God and Father of our Lord Jesus Christ will never leave us 'comfortless'. Is it not this that we are being asked to demonstrate in the harvest of the Spirit? It is a quality that reflects the divine consistency, something that might well be summed up in the modern, and possibly near jargon word — 'commitment'. And commitment? Robert Frost points the direction for us; 'And I have promises to keep . . . and miles to go before I sleep.'

Commitment ignores applause or criticism. It sets aside

money as a determinant of behaviour. It dismisses prestige and position as irrelevancies on the path of life. Commitment means 'pressing toward the mark for the prize of the high calling of God in Christ Jesus'. That involves 'forgetting the things which are behind and reaching forth unto the things which are before' (Philippians 3:13–14). It means 'counting all things but loss' in the search for inner consistency and wholeness.

'Do you see yonder shining light?' Evangelist said to Christian in *Pilgrim's Progress*.
'I think I do,' said Christian.
'Then,' said Evangelist, 'keep that light in your eye.'

The faith, the fidelity that God demands of us is obedience to the Light we have. In other words, commitment.

*   *   *

'I expect to pass through this world but once. Any good therefore that I can do, or any kindness that I can show to my fellow-creature, let me do it now. Let me not defer or neglect it, for I shall not pass this way again.' There is uncertainty about the real source of this quotation — was it Emerson, or Edward Courtney or someone else? but there is no doubt about its validity. Kindness must be shown where and when it can be shown. And kindness is a product in the harvest of the Spirit.

Kindness is, according to the dictionary, a 'disposition to do good to others'. It has compassion in it. Its root points to its appropriateness and its necessity for kindness is 'kin-ness'. It is related to the humanity which man owes to man. It is part of the attitude required within the brotherhood and sisterhood of men and women. It is bound up with the Fatherhood of God. 'Any kindness that I can show . . . let me do it now.'

As with love, patience and joy, the human quality is based on the Divine quality. So is it with kindness. That kindness is, as Professor D. A. Hayes has put it in the Dictionary of the Bible (Hastings, revised by H. H. Rowley and F. C. Grant), 'God's glory stooping to man's need: God's power brought within man's reach, God's mercy and love, as broad as the race, as deep as man's need, as enduring as man's immortality. The Bible reveals it. Jesus manifested it.' 'The philanthropy of God is to be reproduced in the philanthropy of men.'

What then does this imply for us, in practical terms?

First, that the 'trademark' of the Christian community must be compassion. 'Put on the garments that suit God's chosen people, his own, his beloved,' writes Paul to the Colossians (3:12–15, NEB), 'compassion, kindness, humility, gentleness, patience. Be forbearing with one another, and forgiving where any of you has cause for complaint. You must forgive as the Lord forgave you. To crown all, there must be love, to bind all together, and to complete the whole. Let Christ's peace be arbiter in your hearts: to this peace, you were called as members of a single body.'

This is a pattern, as practical as it is profound, for the life of the church. It is almost a check-list by which to test the standards in that part of the Christian community which is 'our' congregation. It is, if we look at the verses immediately preceding clearly set in the context of the universality of the Gospel. 'There is no question here of Greek and Jew, circumcised and uncircumcised, barbarian, Scythian, slave and freeman, but Christ is all and is in all' (verse 11).

Kindness is implicit in the one-ness of mankind. All that destroys this kin-ship is diabolical and forces the Christian into the fight, in the here and now, against racial intolerance and prejudice, the greed which produces 'haves' and 'have-nots', the passions which create war and rumours of war, the unconscious drives, individual and collective, that are expressed in selfishness. We cannot, within the Christian community, speak of kindness without committing ourselves wholeheartedly to the creation of fellowship and unity.

The second, even more practical consequence, is the pressure put on us by the presence of this product in the harvest of the Spirit, to immerse ourselves effectively in the life of the world. The Incarnation is *the* demonstration of the kindness of God. Christ is the Divine kindness manifested to us in human flesh. Our kindness, reflecting this, compels us to involve ourselves in the power structures that decide how and if man shall have a reasonable life.

It is therefore out of this devotional exploration that a philosophy of radical · action, reforming zeal and rebellious grief arises. It is the kindness of God that ultimately pushes us into the very heart of the practical life of the world. And this is as it should be. Reformers have been created by the searing power of kindness and compassion, a compassion born of the kindness of God, nurtured through the Spirit, sanctified (as it must be, otherwise 'power corrupts') by that Holy Spirit.

That 'disposition to do good to others' is truly a product of the harvest of the Spirit. It must always be a disposition expressed in relevant action — to the glory of God and the common good.

*   *   *

The last in the list of qualities mentioned by Paul is, according to the *Authorised Version*, 'temperance'. The rendering of almost all the other versions — certainly *William Barclay, J. B. Phillips, Revised Standard Version, Jerusalem Bible* and the *New English Bible* is 'self-control'.

The theme of this part of the letter to the Galatians is the Christian life as life in the Spirit. Paul sets the central issue of Christian life in the conflict he describes — and

which it is clear he had been very conscious of in himself
— the conflict between 'flesh' and 'spirit'. This is the
perpetual tension as he saw it between our 'lower nature',
the sensual or physical part of our being and our spiritual
hopes and aspirations.

Inherent in the cultural, philosophical and theological
background of Paul's letters are the errors of Gnosticism
and specifically the Gnostic theory of 'duality' — that the
soul is good and the body evil. The soul is accordingly
imprisoned in an evil body. At death that body will,
rightly, be destroyed while the soul will go back to God to
whom it belongs. In our Christian vocabulary something
of these ideas sometimes seems to creep in, for example in
the phrases 'saving our souls', 'the immortality of the
soul', etc. These are not mainstream Christian concepts
but seem to go back nearer to Gnostic ideas, incidentally
much in evidence in contemporary esoteric thinking.
That kind of Gnostic approach led to such excesses as
asceticism, and produced an antinomianism which Paul
often felt bound to attack for it led to a licence of a
fatalistic kind — if the body is evil and to be destroyed, it
does not matter anyway so let us gratify it.

Paul clearly had a different concept of salvation for it
involved the salvation of the whole person, the whole
personality. *We*, not a part of us, live on. So the Christian
creeds significantly talk about belief in the resurrection of
the *body*. Definition of the nature of that resurrection is
very much the subject of Paul's first letter to the
Corinthians (Chapter 15) — 'for the corruptible must put
on incorruption' — as is the whole import of the
section. So there is no question of him seeing the body, as
the Gnostic wisdom did, as wholly evil. But Paul does
clearly see the conflict *within* our personalities between
the lower nature and the demands it makes that culminate
in sexual sins and perversions, idolatry and occult
involvement, violence and inter-personal hostility, heresy,
alcoholic immoderation, etc. (Galatians 5:20–21). It is

precisely in contrast to this he proclaims the harvest of the Spirit and the results it produces.

The concept here is one of balance, as it is in so many areas of Christian belief. 'Seek ye first the Kingdom of God and His righteousness and all these things shall be added unto you' (Matthew 6:33). It is not that the other 'things' are wrong, but they must be contained in proper balance. Put them on the priority side, and we become 'unbalanced'. So with the relationship of 'lower' and 'higher' (or spiritual) natures. If the 'lower nature' dominates and the Spirit takes second place, the result is a living disaster. We shall be led by the 'passions and desires' (Galatians 5:24) of that lower nature into the degradation of our bodies and inevitably, as a result, of our souls. We must therefore 'walk in the Spirit' and allow the Spirit to control our whole being. From that right balance will come the 'harvest of the Spirit'. The aim and indeed spiritual ambition of Christians will then be to reach the stage where the correct balance is achieved between 'flesh' and 'spirit'. It is not that 'flesh', the 'lower nature' or 'the body' is wholly evil and to be set aside, as in the Gnostic emphasis. It is simply that it *must* be under the control of the Spirit. It is the Pauline claim that those who walk in the Spirit do not gratify the desires of the flesh. The Christian is not a 'flesh-dominated' person.

There never is, however, a time when good and evil, right and wrong, flesh and spirit are simple choices. Perhaps of all the conflicts within human experience, this is the one over which aspiring souls have agonised most. 'Self-control' as a concept, is a great ideal, but living in the real world — and particularly in the world of today where the clear landmarks of other ages have disappeared under the welter of new understandings of life and love, some creative, others destructive — has left the Christian to try to be honest with God and honest with himself, in terms of values and standards. The margins are indistinct and the problems real.

One of the most far-reaching changes in this area is the contemporary attitude to the meaning of love. The simple classification of actions and attitudes into 'physical' and 'spiritual' does not meet the genuine feelings of many today. The ultimate 'physical' expression of love, in total togetherness, may well be anything but an act of 'lust', (a word Paul uses a lot) but it is still normally regarded as unacceptable — as cases in recent times, involving priests, nuns and members of churches show. There are many who have not lusted but rather loved, who have been punished severely for their involvement in 'prohibited' relationships.

The concept of 'situation ethics' relates to these kinds of issues. Is there anything that can helpfully be said, that combines faithfulness to the Christian ideal of the dominance of Spirit over flesh with understanding of contemporary situations?

I offer these pointers, and first this one directly from Paul: '*Walk in the Spirit*'. That immediately takes the black/white, 'absolute demand' out of the problem and allows reality, in human terms, to come in. Self-control is an ideal, but progress towards it is a *walk*, a journey, a pilgrimage. The journey will take time and grace, and much learning and insight will come on the way.

The second pointer is, again, that of *balance*. The Christian life, as I said above is not the presence of 'the spiritual' to the *exclusion* of the 'physical'. It lies in balance between them. The correct balance is, as I said before, the one in which 'flesh' is in the care of 'spirit', and not the other way round. There is no doubt which part of us has to be 'in charge'. But to speak as if it were to be wrong to have 'sensual' or 'passionate' feelings or desires is not only unrealistic from a human point of view, it is wrong in itself — and indeed heretical. It is not the Christian view that body, feelings, desires, passion, are wholly part of the kingdom of evil. They are God-given and have a place in true humanity. The issue is solely about balance, perspective and priority. As always on the Christian's map, the balance, perspective and priorities are placed within the equation that says 'Seek ye first the Kingdom of God and his righteousness and other things will be added to you.'

In the *Jerusalem Bible*, there is a note which says that after 'self-control', the phrase 'in Christ Jesus' is added in some manuscripts. Perhaps this is the ultimate clue to it all. 'Self-control' as a mere moral maxim moves in the direction of a legalism and law. It is this that Paul constantly attacks in the Judaisers' approach. In the life of the Spirit, there is less need of law. You only reach the stage of needing no law, however, when you come to be in Christ and so become a 'new creation'. Law restricts, deadens, codifies. Liberty in Christ opens up the possibility of a life of true freedom — not a life of licence, but a life of real liberty. It is within that concept that 'self-control' becomes not negative chains but creative responsibility and true discipline.

There is no doubt that, in Paul's sense, 'self-control' is a product of the harvest of the Spirit. It is the essential discipline that guides the walk in the Spirit in the right direction and towards the right balance.

14

Encouragement, Friendship, Compassion

WE HAVE DISCUSSED briefly the products of the harvest of the Spirit as Paul has given them to us. He has, in his list, covered the basic essential fruits of the working of divine grace in us. I write this chapter — and perhaps after it you will, in thought, want to add your own — in order to add to that list several more products which I feel are also evidence of the presence of the Spirit in life or even add a word more on a product touched on under the main headings, but on which there is more to say.

I begin with *Encouragement*.

There is a very important and fundamental saying of Jesus that makes it imperative that we remember just what we have to do in ministry — ordained or lay. It is the statement in John's Gospel (Chapter 3:17): 'For God sent not His Son into the world to condemn the world, but that the world through Him, might be saved.' This states as clearly as it is possible to do it that the purpose of the Incarnation, Crucifixion and Resurrection is a 'saving' that is a positive, creating undertaking and that God's desire is never to condemn for its own sake. The Gospel therefore has much more to do with *en*couragement than *dis*couragement.

Sadly the church has often taken on the negative role. 'Thou shalt not . . .' has been its proclamation and its effective *modus operandi*. It has shaped its discipline to that end and had people brought before its courts or similar authorities for misdemeanours. It has often not had either the willingness or the patience to try to understand and it has given an impression of judgementalism far outside its own fellowship. Stage caricatures of ecclesiastical figures almost always focus on a negative attitude to aspects of life like smoking, drinking and swearing without any reference to the full life, the life abundant, for which Christianity primarily stands.

The great Scottish preacher, A. J. Gossip, insisted that whatever a sermon had to say, and however 'challenging' it had to be, it should always end with *comfort*. The soothing and strengthening of the troubled soul was and always must be the main object of preaching.

The ministry of our Lord is littered with this quality of encouragement. He is encouraging to the sick, seeking to show them that illness and disease is not God's will (though God may speak through illness when it comes), but that He attacks it always as part of the kingdom of evil. He is encouraging to the victims of society's anger and hostility — tax-gatherer Zacchaeus has the Master as a guest in his house, the woman taken in adultery is not condemned, the woman of bad reputation is praised. He will not send the crowds away. Sheep without a shepherd need care and concern. The one who touched the hem of His garment gained strength.

The gift that enables us to give courage, to en-courage others is of the Spirit and it is one that ought to be expressed corporately too. The church, 'the community of grace' as we have called it, must, because of the access to grace that it has within it, become a climate of grace. Those who come to it must not come fearful that it will only condemn, but believing that it will seek to save. Those who hear of it must hear of its comforting, encouraging attitudes and not only of its negative judgementalism.

Life is full of anxiety, self-pity, fear, struggle and 'problems'. The tensions of the kind of world we live in affect people deeply. Does 'the bomb' or its even more sophisticated successors allow of a future at all? What will happen to children in the educational turmoil of today? Will racial conflict increase and do damage to the society we know? How can we cope with the cost of living now and in the future? How can I live with my secret? How can I face society for if only they knew . . .? The list of questions goes on: the struggle for many is weary, the problems too great. Do I want to live any more in this sort of world? Shall I cut the knot and get out of it all? The opportunity to encourage is all around. Let us not be ashamed of providing it, for in so doing, we shall be reflecting the One who offered the world encouragement — in the name of God, the great Encourager.

God is concerned with life, not death: with salvation not damnation. We are to share the encouragement He offered to the world in Christ who 'lifted up', draws us to Him to make us strong.

*   *   *

Take now the gift of *friendship*. The capacity to offer friendship is a very real fruit of the Spirit.

When Paul talks of the diversity of gifts, he is enunciating the great principle of variety that is part of the evidence of the Spirit's energies. Too often, in Church life and practice, we have tended to limit the variety and diversity of the Divine operation by narrowing the limits to include only certain talents as Spirit-inspired. We have also in our ecclesiastical structures tended to give importance to 'public' gifts that lead to holding office in the church but failed to recognise the more 'private' — that is less publicly seen and valued — gifts.

It is into this 'private' area, the gift of friendship falls. There will be no records kept of its 'success', no statistics to show its blessings, but of its value in the eyes of God there can be no doubt. It is a gift the Master had and would wish on His disciples.

Another principle Paul laid down was the peculiarity of gifts to people. We are not all equally gifted. 'In each of us the Spirit is manifested in one particular way for some useful purpose. One man, through the Spirit, has the gift of wise speech, while another, by the power of the same Spirit, is granted faith; another by the one Spirit, gifts of healing, and another miraculous powers; another has the gift of prophecy, and another the ability to distinguish true spirits from false: yet another has the gift of ecstatic utterance of different kinds, and another the ability to interpret it. But all these gifts are the work of one and the same Spirit, distributing them severally to each individual at will' (I Corinthians 12:7–11). It is not therefore any denigration of us if we show we are gifted in only one way, or several ways rather than in everything. This is how God works.

This brings an egalitarianism into the possession of gifts that is salutary. Ecclesiastical status may be important to men and women but 'status symbols mean nothing to God' (Galatians 2:6 WB). The more public gifts represented in a church — musical, financial supervision, organisational leadership, property skills — are as important as, but ultimately no more important than more private gifts like the ability to offer friendship, the capacity to make tea, a sense of humour, a reconciling presence.

This, unfortunately, church organisation and leadership is slow to recognise and the more 'private' people with their gifts, are not used as they might be. The extrovert finds himself with public offices heaped on him while the retiring, reticent, quiet, shy introvert is not seen to be gift-laden. Yet in the apostolic company, both played a part. The extrovert Peter certainly moved inexorably to a leadership position but the introvert Andrew was the medium of introduction (as in the case of the Greeks who 'came to see Jesus'). He may have immediately put them in touch with Peter, but it is perhaps no accident that they were attracted to Andrew as the doorway to meeting Christ.

The capacity to make friends and to offer real friendship is not everybody's gift. Some, perhaps to our surprise, find the ability to relate at deeper levels is not part of their equipment. In social, 'cocktail party' situations where there is no demand and the situation is ephemeral, they have no problem, but pushed to offer more than casual interest, their ability to relate is found wanting and their capacity for deep friendship shown to be limited. In my experience of church life, it is often the comparatively unknown and publicly unsung who may be strongest in this talent. And when that gift is recognised, the church has found an asset. Our Lord Himself knew and publicly recognised the gift and value of those with a capacity for friendship. We must never classify this talent as other than extraordinary. It is a sign of grace and is of immense value to the Kingdom.

*   *   *

To *add* the word 'compassion' to the list of Paul's fruits of the Spirit would certainly be unfair! It is a part of Love, and under that heading it has of course been mentioned. But it is such an important fruit of the great harvest and is so relevant in our contemporary thinking and acting, that I take a little space to develop the theme of compassion now.

Recall the verses from Mark that I quoted earlier.

'And Jesus, moved with compassion for him, put forth His hand . . .'

'When He saw the multitudes, He was moved with compassion on them. . . .'

Behind all healing attitudes, there lies 'compassion'. Nowhere is this divine attribute more beautifully summed up than in the phrase 'moved with compassion'. It points to the very heart of God and, reaching there, demonstrates the nature of God. The God of Jesus Christ has compassion in His heart and at His heart.

Efforts in other translations to vary this phrase (and

sometimes translators seem to feel that they must, at all costs, never use *Authorised Version* phrases, however good!) fail to express this divine attitude as well as 'moved with compassion' does. 'With warm indignation', in the *New English Bible* version of the first verse above, falls short. The second verse I have quoted sounds a little better . . . 'Moved to pity'. 'Moved to pity' and 'He had compassion' come from the *Revised Standard Version*. 'He felt sorry' and 'feeling sorry' are the *Jerusalem Bible's* contributions. 'Filled with pity' and 'deeply moved with pity' come from *J. B. Phillips*.

In the end, I go back to that *Authorised Version* translation of so long ago as the most inspired of all: Jesus was 'moved with compassion'. That phrase says almost everything that needs to be said about the nature of God.

Compassion is, by derivation, a 'suffering with' someone as I said under 'Love'. Yet it is a quality more than sympathy or even empathy, both of which might be described in those terms. It is the understanding of and, as far as possible, the sharing of suffering in 'feeling' terms, but it recognises the limits to our ability to feel realistically what the sufferer feels. The pain someone bears is, and can only be, their pain. To enter into it and feel it as it is being felt, lies beyond our normal human ability. The feelings and thoughts of those who, in human terms, are incurably ill, can draw forth our sympathy and our sincere attempts at empathy, but it is not easy and perhaps not even possible for the sympathiser to feel just what being in that position does to attitudes, relationships and ways of living.

Compassion goes one step further than sympathy or empathy usually do, just because there is an element of being 'moved' in the deepest places in it. We are impelled to an expression of some kind of action, however limited that action can be. In the case of the 'him' in the first verse quoted, Jesus 'stretched forth His hand and touched him' and the leper was cleansed. In the case of the 'them' in the second verse, He responded by the appointment of the disciples 'to cast out devils and to cure every kind of ailment and disease'. *Compassion results in action of some kind* . . . a touch, an embrace, a kiss, a decision . . . because the inner heart has been 'moved'.

The feeling of compassion welling up is a distinctive one and a recognisable one. It happens in situations that, for some reason not necessarily definable, have the capacity to touch the deep places, to graze the soul, to create love. The feelings are subjective, yet their compassionate characteristic is their objectivity. This is not the love that identifies in a way that brings 'emotional involvement' (if I may repeat a point or two from the earlier chapters). It is not the love that moves on to a relationship of shorter or longer duration. It is a love which carries no implications beyond the compassion it feels. It does not necessarily imply any 'on-going' responsibility. It is the outflow of the moment, in response to need or pain or suffering or bereavement or hurt. Sincerely offered, it brings the blessing of the moment. Having been given from the soul, in that moment, and expressed in whatever 'action' is appropriate, we move on to the next thing we have to do, the next moment that may move to compassion again.

Our moments of compassion may come seldom or often, but when they do, they are expressing something which is of the healing attitude of God Himself. Be glad when you are 'moved to compassion'. It is a sign of the presence of the healing Spirit in you.

15

Empathy, Humour, Tea-making

MUCH HAS BEEN written and said in Christian circles about sympathy. Perhaps one of the other fruits of the Spirit that is specially relevant in days when so much help comes through relationship is the word Empathy, the relationship of understanding that enables us to enter into another's suffering. Compassion we have just described as that step that comes out of true empathy.

We begin with the divine empathy which is so perfectly described in Hebrews 4, verse 15 (WB): 'Jesus, the Son of God . . . is not a high priest who is unable to sympathise with the weaknesses that we possess . . . in every respect (He) has gone through the same ordeal of temptation as we have to go through . . .'

That verse states the divine empathy in all its glory. That verse about God's attitude to our failure should touch us deeply and make us glad.

It is the experience of every pastor in relation to his people that temptation and acceding to temptation so often bring agony of soul.

Wilt thou forgive that sinne where I begunne
Which is my sinne, though it were done before?
Wilt thou forgive those sinnes through which I runne,
And do run still: though still I do deplore?
When thou has done, thou hast not done
For I have more

Wilt thou forgive that sinne by which I have wonne
Others to sin, and made my sinne their doore?
Wilt thou forgive that sinne which I did shunne
A yeare, or two: but wallowed in, a score? When thou
has done, thou hast not done,
For I have more.

How easy it is to feel the truth of John Donne's words as he looks into his life and soul, for there goes every one of us. Guilt is the bugbear of so many, yet guilt there should be. It is right to feel guilt when we fall short of standards, God's or our own. It would be wrong if no guilt were felt over sin committed. But a guilt which is appropriate is one thing. What is a pastor's concern is the guilt which is so deeply rooted that nothing can be done to achieve some ease ... not even a real sense of the reality of the divine forgiveness.

Setting aside the problem of pathological guilt which may require deeper understanding of the human condition behind it, a true and proper sense of guilt can still bring inner turmoil. The more sensitive a soul is to the feeling of having 'sinned against God', the more feelings of guilt will bring interior agony.

It is here that a sense of the reality of the divine empathy brings healing. Temptation is not peculiar to us. Sin is common to all mankind, for as I quoted earlier, 'there is none righteous, no not one ... all have sinned and come short of the glory of God'. But what is much more important is that it is also part of the divine experience. And in a real way. The sins faced by God-made-man (as I have said before) are less likely to be the ones that trouble ordinary humanity most ... such as sins of behaviour in relationship, whether of a sexual, bitter or unrighteously angry kind. The abuse of divine power was the focal point of Satan's attack on Christ. But the experience is of the same kind: the inner pressure to accede, the struggle during the sinning, the remorse and regret afterwards. Whether it be temper lost, bitterness expressed or failure of a physical kind, all sensitive to the Spirit will know the agony that brought tears of remorse to Peter and suicide to Judas. How easily that awful extreme can make its presence felt when temptation is past and sin is complete. Go on, with John Donne, but go right to the end:

I have a sinne of feare, that when I have spunne
My last thread, I shall perish on the shore;
Sweare by thy selfe that at my death thy sonne
Shall shine as he shines now and heretofore:
And having done that, Thou haste done.
I feare no more.

Behind the divine empathy is the divine consistency. The understanding of God, through His own experience in Christ, becomes the forgiveness of God, 'until seventy times seven' with its continuous acceptance.

The divine empathy must be reflected in the pastor. He/she is human too. He/she has wrestled in agony with temptation too. He/she has gone under too . . . perhaps repeatedly ('For I have more'). He/she has known the remorse, the regret, the agony of failure too and perhaps even the more so because of 'special position'.

It is worrying to see the harshness of judgement and attitude 'the church' sometimes shows to those who wrestle with temptation, for it does not represent the God we know through Christ. Let those who are called to pastoral ministry for ever dwell on that awe-inspiring phrase already quoted, 'There but for the grace of God, go I'. And if indeed they have gone through the fire themselves, let them count it some kind of privilege, for under the grace of God, they will have learned the full meaning of empathy and its part in the redemption of the people.

And they will be reflecting that empathy which is Divine.

*   *   *

I feel I cannot reach the end of these additional products of the harvest of the Spirit without including the possibility that a sense of humour is a symptom of the presence of the Spirit.

There is, The Preacher (Ecclesiastes) reminds us, 'a time to laugh'. It is not all the time, for there are times to weep. The sensitivity that comes through the presence of the Spirit will determine when humour is an asset and when it is out of place. There are some who try to turn the whole of life into a joke — which it is not. The humourist who dodges life's problems through the joker's special defence — flippancy, reveals his inability to face his or her problems. There is many a potential leader who has lost the opportunity to lead through flippancy where seriousness was appropriate.

Tony Monopoly, the contemplative monk turned pop-singer, said, in a television interview, that you could not be such a monk without a sense of humour. He is probably right. It is certainly my experience to find that some of the saints of God who have suffered grievously have the most active sense of fun. As Fernandel in his role of Don Camillo showed so attractively, our relationship with God and the way He treats us often touch off wry commentary on the mysterious way God moves 'His wonders to perform'.

In the life of faith, as in the life of the church, the gift of a sense of humour can be a huge asset. There is nothing in religious belief or faith that says our sense of fun should be destroyed. The humour that helps, the smiles that enhance, the laugh that breaks the tension relevantly are, I have no doubt, a result of the 'smiling face' of God working through His Spirit.

It would be wrong to turn our Lord into the great Humourist, as wrong as it would be to turn Him into the great Socialist, Conservative, Psychotherapist or any of the many other 'ists' that have been heaped on Him, but it does look as if in many of His statements, images and actions, there was a sense of humour. (Alec McCowen, in his public rendering from memory of the *Authorised Version* of St. Mark's Gospel and the amusement associated with the parables in the musical *Godspell* are two reminders of how much humour can be drawn from the Gospels). If some Christian disciple, with a laugh in his heart, can ease the hurt of the world, is it not of God?

I like to think so and therefore include, not all humour by a long way, but true humour certainly somewhere in this extended list of the harvest of the Spirit.

*   *   *

By the way, almost, of epilogue, I add just one more product of the Spirit. It is the ability to make and serve a 'good cup of tea'.

In every church, without fail, there are those who do no more than make the tea. But should one even use words like 'just' or phrases like 'no more than' in this context, for to do this demands a gift that goes deeply into the heart of Christian faith and practice. The 'tea-makers' take us back to the very source of Christianity.

There was a night they gathered — Our Lord and His friends — to have a last meal together. 'When the even was come, He sat down with the twelve ... and ... they did eat ...'. But who made the meal, set out the food and wine, served it, washed up? We do not know. We only know it was all prepared in advance. Whoever made that meal had an anonymous, but crucial part in the foundation and continuity of the church of Christ. To 'such a man' who had been asked to give his room and to those who helped prepare the table of the Lord came the privilege and honour of participating in the founding of the sacramental life of the church.

So those who feel they can offer this gift stand in a great tradition. And who shall say such love and care and talent is not a fruit in the harvest of the Spirit?

EPILOGUE

The Pilgrimage of Grace

WE HAVE TAKEN our journey through the inner silence to the harvest of the Spirit. It has been a simple exposition of aspects of the Christian life and the source of the power to live it creatively. I have taken as fundamental to all that I have said the Christian stance — 'within the faith', the Christian 'map' — which has a perspective based on the primacy of the spiritual and the initiative of God in the process of growth and development towards wholeness. I have emphasised the need for our waiting on God in the silence in order that the miracle of grace may be effected and the seeds of the sanctified life be planted and nurtured. I have indicated some of the ways in which Christian qualities may emerge in the grace-full man or woman.

I have also emphasised the strength of the 'opposing forces' within, a strength that every honest believer will acknowledge. I have noted that the pressure from 'evil' grows stronger the *more* we grow in grace. So life becomes a pilgrimage of grace in which there is always hope, just because the struggle is not one we have to face alone. God is in the struggle, actively not passively and with understanding.

I am therefore in effect simply restating fundamental Christian belief as it has been expressed in creed or credo. I believe 'in God, the Father, Almighty, Maker of heaven and earth, and of all things visible and invisible'. God is at the centre. The map is theocentric. The power of creation and development is His, just as the initiative in creation and redemption is His. It is because 'He first loved us' that we respond in love with worship.

'I believe in Jesus Christ, our Lord, God of God'. The stance is Christ-centred. All our looking is to Him of whom we say with Peter, in that moment of profound revelation (for 'flesh and blood' had no part in making it known) 'Thou art the Christ, the Son of the living God'. So the 'pre-existent', incarnate, crucified, risen and ascended Christ is the focus of the new creation, for it is in and through Him, the miracle of grace begins.

'I believe in "the Holy Spirit . . . the Giver of Life",' promised in the words of Christ, received by the first disciples at Pentecost and ever energising the life of the aspirant to wholeness. The creative silence is the meeting place of soul with Spirit and through the grace bestowed, the harvest of the Spirit comes.

The experience of faith — the meeting with God in Christ through the Spirit — is the experience of the ages, authenticated by the church in the Word of God. It is the experience known today and every day by those who come, receptive to the Spirit. The harvest of the Spirit is evidence of the Triune God working to integrate believers and make them whole.

That passage in the letter to the Ephesians (3:14–21, NEB) sums it all up.

> With this in mind, then, I kneel in prayer to the Father, from whom every family in heaven and on earth takes its name, that out of the treasures of his glory he may grant you strength and power through His Spirit in your inner being, that through faith Christ may dwell in your hearts in love. With deep roots and firm foundations, may you be strong to grasp, with all God's people, what is the breadth, length, depth and height of the love of Christ, and to know it, though it is beyond knowledge. So may you attain to fullness of being, the fullness of God Himself.
>
> Now to Him who is able to do immeasurably more than all we can ask or conceive, by the power which is at work among us, to Him be

glory in the church and in Christ Jesus from generation to generation evermore!   Amen

APPENDIX

The following Meditations may be of help to those who want to engage in regular and deepening Meditation. They were nearly all used by the author in a Meditation Group which met in London for some six years. In that Group these Meditations would last for 40–45 minutes. As time went on, fewer words were used, sometimes only two phrases. But in the early stages of the Group's life some structure was found helpful.

The spaces between the phrases or sentences indicate periods of silent dwelling on the theme. The Meditations can be used over periods of from 15 minutes to one hour. Biblical references are to the *Authorised Version* unless otherwise stated.

WINGS
(based on Isaiah 40:31; Psalm 57:1; Mal. 4:2;
Andrew Reed)

'They that wait upon the Lord . . .
    shall mount up with wings . . .'

THE WINGS OF DIVINE INSPIRATION

'I will make my refuge in the shadow of thy wings'

THE WINGS OF DIVINE PROVIDENCE

'How often would I have gathered thy children together,
    as a hen doth gather her brood under her wings'

THE WINGS OF DIVINE COMPASSION

'The Sun of Righteousness shall arise
    with healing in his wings'

THE WINGS OF DIVINE HEALING

'Come as the Dove and spread thy wings,
    the wings of peaceful love'

Amen

THE DAYSPRING
(based on St. Luke 1:78–79, *Authorised Version* and *New English Bible*)

'The Dayspring from on high hath visited us'

THE DAWN HAS BROKEN

'In the tender compassion of our God'

IT IS GOD'S GIFT

'To shine on those who live in darkness'

TO THOSE IN NEED

'To give light to those in the shadow of death'

AND IN DESPAIR

'To guide our feet into the way of peace'

AND TO ALL WHO SEEK

Amen

THE GLORY OF LIFE

The Glory of Life

is

to love . . .

to give . . .

To be a strong hand in the dark to another in time of need . . .

To be a cup of strength to any soul in a crisis of weakness . . .

This is to know

THE GLORY OF LIFE

Amen

This Meditation is based on an anonymous poem on the wall of Alida Bosshardt's room in the Goodwill Centre in Amsterdam's red light district. It is the room from which Colonel Bosshardt of the Salvation Army has exercised her ministry in that area for the past 26 years. Her story is told in *Here is my Hand* (by Denis Duncan, paperback Hodder & Stoughton).

THE RIVER OF LIFE
(based on Revelation 22:1–2)

'And he showed me a pure river of

WATER OF LIFE'

'On either side of the river was the

TREE OF LIFE'

The river of the water of life had its

SOURCE IN GOD HIMSELF

'proceeding out of the throne of God and of the Lamb'

'And the leaves of the tree were for the

HEALING OF THE NATIONS'

Amen

LIFE RENEWED
(based on Psalm 23, *New English Bible*)

'The Lord is my shepherd'

'He makes me lie down in green pastures'
HE GIVES TO MY BODY

'He leads me beside the waters of peace'
HE GIVES TO MY MIND

'He renews life within me'
HE GIVES TO MY SOUL

And so 'He leads me in the right path'

'Goodness and Love unfailing . . . will follow me
    all the days of my life'

'I shall want nothing'

And these, the Shepherd's blessings, I ask
FOR ALL

Amen

126

A NEW SONG
(based on Psalm 40:1–3, *New English Bible*)

I waited, waited for the Lord . . .

He bent down to me . . .

He heard my cry . . .

He brought me up . . .

He set my feet on a rock . . .

He gave me a firm footing . . .

On my lips, he put a new song . . .

'Thanks be to God, who giveth us the victory
through our Lord, Jesus Christ'

Amen

WASHED ...

(based on Psalm 51:7, *New English Bible*; St. John 13:1–7,
New English Bible; St. Luke 7:36–50, *Authorised Version*;
Revelation 7:14, *Authorised Version*)

'Wash me, that I may become whiter than snow'

Our Prayer for Cleansing

'If I your Lord and Master have washed your feet,
you also ought to wash one another's feet'

Our Prayer for Humility

'But she hath washed my feet with tears'

Our Prayer for Greater Love

'These are they which have come out of great
tribulation and have washed their robes and
made them white ...'

Our Prayer for those who suffer

Amen

DEEP ROOTS
(based on Ephesians 3:18, *New English Bible*)

Let your focal point be
A TREE

growing . . .

   spreading . . .

      living . . .

It has leaves . . . branches . . . trunk . . .
But its life comes from its
ROOTS

That life will be more secure with
DEEP ROOTS

Its life is fed by rain . . . sun . . . wind . . .
   resources from outside, given to enable growth

We are as
TREES

We need resources from outside of us . . .
   the warmth of people, the wind of the Spirit

Then we can push down
DEEP ROOTS

From these roots we
   GROW . . . into Faith
      REACH UP . . . in Hope
         SPREAD OUT . . . in Love

              Amen

WIDE-AWAKE GOD
(based on Psalm 121, *New English Bible* and
Psalm 139:18, *Authorised Version*)

'I lift up my eyes to the hills...'

'Help comes from the Lord . . .'

'How could he let your foot stumble?'

'How could he, your guardian, sleep?'

God 'never slumbers, never sleeps'

And 'when I awake, I am still with thee'

'The Lord is your guardian . . .'

'He will guard you, body and soul'

Amen

GOD WITH US
(based on St. John 1:1–14 and St. Matthew 1:23)

In the beginning . . .
was the

WORD

The Word was with

GOD

The Word was

GOD

In him was

LIFE

And the life was the

LIGHT

of men

The Word was made

FLESH

and dwelt among us
and they shall call his name

EMMANUEL

which means

GOD WITH US

Amen

RECONCILIATION
(based on II Corinthians 5:17–20, *New English Bible*)

In a divided, war-torn, prejudiced world,
     there are, nevertheless, some symbols of
     reconciliation.
          On these we can focus with hope

The Christ of the Andes

The Reconciliation Centre near Dublin

A united Communion Service

'God was in Christ, reconciling the world to himself'

'Be reconciled to God'

'He has entrusted us with the message of Reconciliation'

'When anyone is united to Christ, there is a new
     creation'

'We are ambassadors for Christ', bearing the 'word of
reconciliation'

                    Amen

THE VINE
(based on St. John 15:1–7)

I am the vine

You are the branches

Without me, you can do nothing

Abide in Me

If you abide in me,
    You shall ask what you will
        And it shall be done unto you

Amen

THE HOLY SPIRIT
(based on John 14:26)

Come Holy Spirit . . .

Come . . .

The Comforter

which is the Holy Ghost,

whom the Father will send in my name,

He shall teach you all things

And bring all things to your remembrance

Whatsoever I have said unto you

Come, Holy Spirit . . .

Come . . .

Come . . .

Come . . .

Amen

LOVE (1)
(based on I Corinthians 13, *William Barclay* version)

If I am without Love

I am nothing

Love is patient

Love is kind

Love never does the graceless thing

Love's first instinct is to believe in people

Love lasts for ever

Amen

JESUS, LORD

Jesus is LORD

Jesus IS Lord

JESUS is Lord

LORD JESUS

Amen

THE SUFFERING SERVANT
(based on Isaiah 53 and John 12:32)

Surely he hath borne our griefs

   and carried our sorrows

He was wounded for our transgressions

He was despised and rejected, a man of sorrows

'But I, if I be lifted up from the earth

   will draw all men unto Me'

                              Amen

I AM . . .
(based on John 14:6)

I am the Way

I am the Truth

I am the Life

Amen

THE GIFT
(based on John 3:16)

God so loved the world that

He gave his only begotten Son

that whosoever believeth in him

should not perish but

have everlasting life

Thanks be to God

Amen

LOVE (2)
(based on I John 4:7 and 16)

Love is of God

God is Love

Amen

NON NOBIS, DOMINE......

Hallelujah!

Hallelujah!

HALLELUJAH!

Amen